THE BOOK OF
SONGS & RHYMES
WITH BEAT MOTIONS

Keeping the Beat

REVISED EDITION

G-5879

THE BOOK OF
SONGS & RHYMES
with BEAT MOTIONS

Keeping the Beat

REVISED EDITION

Compiled by John M. Feierabend

GIA PUBLICATIONS, INC. · CHICAGO

G-5879
The Book of Songs and Rhymes with Beat Motions (Revised Edition)
Compiled by John M. Feierabend
www.giamusic.com/feierabend

Artwork: Tim Phelps
Editor: Lillie Feierabend
Layout: Nina Fox

Copyright © 2020, 2004
GIA Publications, Inc.
7404 S. Mason Avenue
Chicago, IL 60638

Table of
Contents

Introduction 7

Follow the Child's Beat 9

Follow the Child's Beat Using Instruments 24

Stationary Beat 33

Stationary Circles 55

    Passing Objects 72

    Passing the Beat 79

Beats in Groups of 2 & 3 81

    Beats in 2 84

    Beats in 3 90

Traveling but Not in a Circle 97

Traveling Circle Games 111

Simple Dances 131

Introduction

I t feels great to get into the rhythm of the beat. Children and adults have been doing it for generations. This book contains songs, rhymes, and games that encourage moving with the beat.

All of the songs and rhymes in this book have been passed down from generation to generation and are full of wonder, magic, and make-believe.

Establishing a feeling for the beat is central to all later rhythmic development. These activities are ideal for helping children become proficient at feeling the beat.

This collection includes beat games where the song or rhyme follows the child's preferred beat tempo, games where everyone stays in one place and the beat is felt in hand movements, as well as activities where the beat is put in the feet as everyone travels around the room.

These childhood games help develop a feeling for the beat that will last a lifetime, whether dancing at a wedding or clapping in time with everyone during a sporting event.

So, come on in and play these games. Feeling the beat feels great!

John M. Feierabend

FOLLOW THE CHILD'S BEAT

Ambos a Dos *Puerto Rican*

Am - bos a dos, Ma - ta - ri - le, ri - le, ri - le, Am -
bos a dos, Ma - ta - ri - le, ri - le, rón. Now
what can you do, Ma - ta - ri - le, ri - le, ri - le? Now
what can you do, Ma - ta - ri - le, ri - le, rón? Now
we can do it too, Ma - ta - ri - le, ri - le, ri - le. Now
we can do it too, Ma - ta - ri - le, ri - le, rón.

Motions

The group forms a circle. During the first two lines, one child walks around the inside of the circle. During lines three and four, the child in the center demonstrates a motion with the beat. During the last two lines, the group imitates that motion.

Dame Get Up

Dame get up— and bake your pies,
bake your pies, bake your pies.
Dame get up— and bake your pies on
this fine day in the morn - ing.

Motions

Have all the children simultaneously pantomime some motion involved in making a pie. All should sing at the same tempo. Have each child take a turn pantomiming a motion involved in making a pie. Have the class imitate the motion while singing the song at the tempo set by the child.

Hey, Betty Martin

Hey, Bet - ty Mar - tin, tip - toe, tip - toe,

Hey, Bet - ty Mar - tin, tip - toe fine.

Hey, Bet - ty Mar - tin, tip - toe, tip - toe,

Fine

Hey, Bet - ty Mar - tin, please be mine.

(Jump) with me, I'll (jump) with you.

We'll go (jump-ing) the whole day through.

(Jump) so fine, (jump) so fine.

D.C. al Fine

(Jump - ing,) (jump - ing) all the time.

Motions

Children tip-toe around in a circle with
one child in the center. During the second
half of the song, the child in the center
demonstrates a motion and all children
imitate that motion. At the end of the
song, the child in the center chooses
another to be in the center.

Did You Ever See a Lassie?

Did you ev - er see a las - sie, a las-sie, a las-sie? Did you
(lad - die)

ev - er see a las - sie go this way and that? Go
(lad - die)

this way and that way, go this way and that way. Did you

ev - er see a las - sie go this way and that?
(lad - die)

Motions

The group forms a circle. The child in the center shows a motion during the first two lines. The group imitates the motion during the last two lines.

Do, Do, Pity My Case

Do, do, pi-ty my case, In some la-dy's gar-den, My

clothes to wash when I get home, In some la-dy's gar-den.

Motions

The children stand in a circle. They take turns thinking of some chore and pantomiming a motion to represent that chore. All children imitate that motion and sing the song at the appropriate tempo to reflect the motion.

Down in the Valley

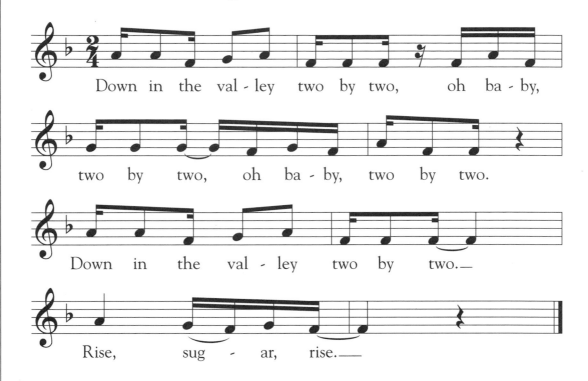

Down in the val - ley two by two, oh ba - by,

two by two, oh ba - by, two by two.

Down in the val - ley two by two. —

Rise, sug - ar, rise. ——

Additional Verses & Motions

Begin with an odd number of children. All children find a partner. The odd one out goes to the center of the circle.

Verse 1

Children walk around in a circle two by two.

Verse 2

Let me see you make a motion, two by two...

The circle stops. The child in the center shows a motion. The group imitates that motion.

Verse 3

Choose another partner, two by two...

For younger children - Children scatter around and find a new partner and rejoin the circle. The remaining child goes to the center.

For older children - The outside circle goes in one direction, and the inside circle goes in the opposite direction. The one in the middle joins the inside circle. At the end of the song, everyone stops and grabs a partner. The one remaining goes to the center.

Haul Away Joe

Way, haul a - way, We'll haul and sing to - geth - er.—

Way, haul a - way,— we'll haul a - way Joe.

Motions

Ask individuals to pantomime motions that represent various chores that would need to be done on a ship. As each child shows his or her motion, sing the song following that child's tempo.

My Mother Sent Me Unto You

My moth - er sent me un - to you.

What to do? What to do? My

moth - er sent— me un - to you, To

do— with one as I do; To

do— with one as I do.

Motions

*Each child takes a turn showing motions
while the rest of the children imitate those
motions. The group should follow the
tempo set by the leader.*

Puncinella

Verse 1

Look who is here, Pun - cin - el - la, Pun - cin - el - la,

Look who is here Pun - cin - el - la in the shoe! Now,

Verse 2

What can you do, Pun - cin - el - la, Pun - cin - el - la?

What can you do, Pun - cin - el - la in the shoe?

Verse 3

Now we can do it too, Puncinella,
  Puncinella,
We can do it too, Puncinella in the
  shoe.

Verse 4

Now who do you choose, Puncinella,
  Puncinella?
Who do you choose, Puncinella in
  the shoe?

Motions

*Children stand in a circle. One child
(Puncinella) stands in the center.
Verse 1: The child in the center walks
around the inside of the circle.
Verse 2: The child in the center performs
some repetitive motion on the beat.
Verse 3: All children copy that motion.
Verse 4: The child in the center covers his
or her eyes with one hand and turns
pointing with the other hand. When the
verse ends, "Puncinella" and the child to
whom he or she is pointing trade places
and the game repeats from the beginning.*

Rock Candy

Rock can - dy ev - 'ry day, Rock can - dy ev - 'ry day,

Rock can - dy ev - 'ry day, Do your own rock can - dy!

Motions

*The children stand in a circle. One child
in the center makes some motion on the
beat. All children copy that motion as they
sing the second verse.*

Verse 2

We can do it, yes we can,
We can do it, yes we can,
We can do it, yes we can,
Do your own rock candy!

Santa Maloney

Here we go San - ta Ma - lo - ney,

Here we go San - ta Ma - lo - ney,

Here we go San - ta Ma - lo - ney as

we go 'round a - bout.

Motions

Children walk around in a circle during the song. At the end of the song, the circle stops and a child performs a motion that all children imitate following that child's tempo. Sing words approriate to the action such as, "Tap your hand on your knee." Then sing the original song again while walking around in a circle. Continue repeating the song until each child has had a turn to suggest a motion.

The Farmer

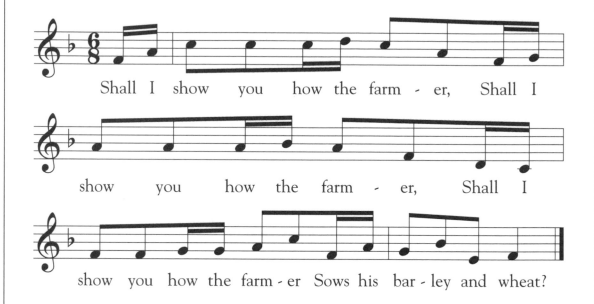

Shall I show you how the farm - er, Shall I show you how the farm - er, Shall I show you how the farm - er Sows his bar - ley and wheat?

Additional Verses

2. Look, it's so, so that the farmer,
Look, it's so, so that the farmer,
Look, it's so, so that the farmer
Sows his barley and wheat.

3. Shall I show you how the
farmer...Mows his barley and wheat?

4. Look it's so, so, how the
farmer...Mows his barley and wheat.

5. Shall I show you how the
farmer...Harvests barley and wheat?

6. Look it's so, so, how the
farmer...Harvests barley and wheat.

7. Shall I show you how the
farmer...Threshes barley and wheat?

8. Look it's so, so, how the
farmer...Threshes barley and wheat.

Motions

One child in the center of the circle sings all odd numbered verses while demonstrating a motion. The rest of the children sing the even numbered verses imitating the center child's motion and tempo.

The Monkey Stomps His Feet

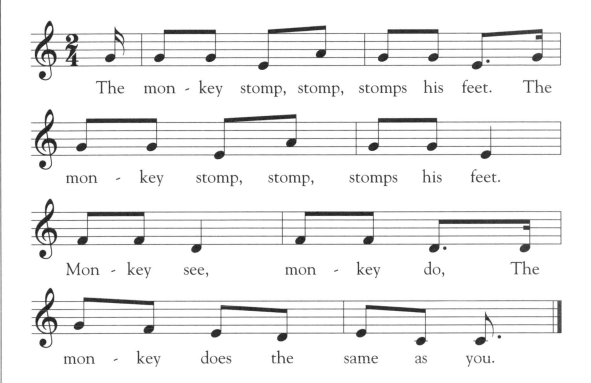

The mon - key stomp, stomp, stomps his feet. The
mon - key stomp, stomp, stomps his feet.
Mon - key see, mon - key do, The
mon - key does the same as you.

Motions

Children stand in a circle with one child in the center. The child in the center performs some motion and the group copies the motion following that child's tempo.

FOLLOW THE CHILD'S BEAT

Using Instruments

Fiddlers Playing

Fid - dlers play - ing, fid - dlers play - ing,

come and dance now.

Tam - bou - rines are gen - tly play - ing,

come and dance now.

We will dance the whole day through,

Sing - ing as we're danc - ing too.

Come and dance now.

Motions

Invite students, one at a time, to tap the beat on a tambourine.
The teacher should sing the song at the tempo set by the student.

Hickory, Dickory, Dock

Hickory, dickory, dock.
The mouse ran up the clock.
The clock struck one, the mouse ran
    down,
Hickory, dickory, dock.

Motions

Invite students, one at a time, to keep the beat with a wood block. The teacher should chant the poem at the tempo set by the student.

Engine, Engine

Engine, Engine Number Nine,
Running down Chicago Line.
See it sparkle, see it shine,
Engine, Engine Number Nine.

Motions

Invite students, one at a time, to keep the beat with the sandblocks. The teacher should chant the poem at the tempo set by the student.

When I Was a Shoemaker

When I was a shoe-mak-er and a shoe-ma-ker was I; A

this-a-way and a that-a-way and a this-a-way went I.

Motions

One child (the leader) suggests a motion to perform on the beat.
Everyone copies that motion and sings the song at the tempo set
by the leader.

or

Invite students, one at a time, to keep the beat with the claves.
The teacher should sing the song at the tempo set by the student.

William He Had Seven Sons

Wil-liam he had sev-en sons, sev-en sons, sev-en sons.

Wil-liam he had sev-en sons and this is what they did.

Motions

Individuals suggest different motions to perform on the beat.
The class performs those motions to the tempo determined by
the individual.
or
Invite students, one at a time, to strum the beat on an autoharp
(teacher holds down the F chord button). The teacher should
sing the song at the tempo set by the student.

Frog in the Meadow

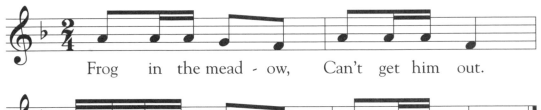

Frog in the mead - ow, Can't get him out.

Take a lit - tle stick and stir him a - bout.

Motions

Invite students, one at a time, to keep the beat with the guiro.
The teacher should sing the song at the tempo set by the student.

Listen, Listen

Lis - ten, lis - ten, Here I come;

Some - one spe - cial gets the drum.

Motions

Invite students, one at a time, to keep the beat with the drum.
The teacher should sing the song at the tempo set by the student.

Cobbler, Cobbler

Cob - bler, cob - bler, mend my shoe.

Have it done by half past two.

Tu - ra - lu - ra - lu.

Half past two is much too late,

Have it done by half past eight.

Tu - ra - lu - ra - lu.

Motions

Invite students, one at a time, to tap the beat with the claves. The teacher should sing the song at the tempo set by the student.

There's a Cobbler

There's a cobbler down the street
Mending shoes for little feet;
With a bang and a bang and a bang,
　bang, bang,
And a bang and a bang and a bang,
　bang, bang.

Mending shoes the whole day long,
Mending shoes to make them strong;
With a bang and a bang and a bang,
　bang, bang,
And a bang and a bang and a bang,
　bang, bang.

Motions

*Invite students, one at a time, to tap the
beat with the claves. The teacher should
chant the poem at the tempo set by the
student.*

STATIONARY BEAT

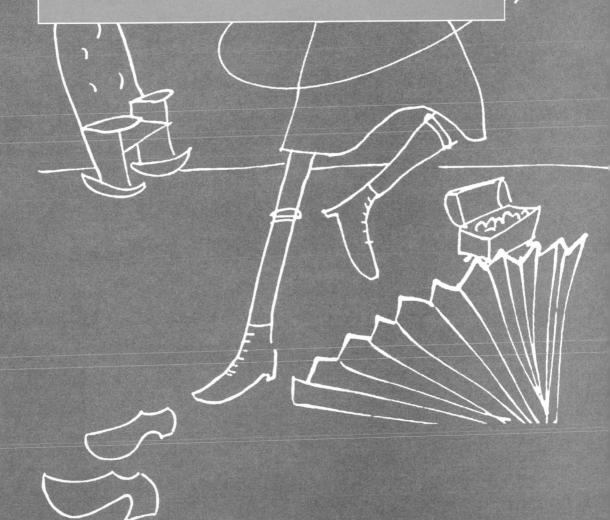

Aiken Drum   *Scottish*

There was a man lived in the moon, lived
in the moon, lived in the moon. There
was a man lived in the moon and his
name was Ai - ken Drum.

Additional Verses & Motions

During the first verse, the group taps with the beat on their legs. Ask the group what Aiken Drum's head could be made of. Draw that object on a blackboard or large piece of paper. Have the class tap with the beat on their heads while singing:

And his head was made of _____, of _____, of _____,
And his head was made of _____,
And his name was Aiken Drum.

After head try:

Body, legs, arms, eyes, nose, and mouth.

Ask what other body parts could be made of. Draw that body part and sing while tapping on that body part.

Maybe add hands, feet, fingers, and toes.

When finished drawing "the man in the moon," sing the first verse one more time while tapping on legs.

Aserrín *Latin American*

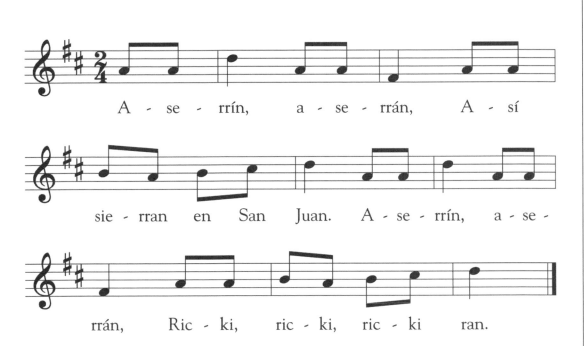

A - se - rrín,   a - se - rrán,   A - sí

sie - rran   en   San   Juan.   A - se - rrín,   a - se -

rrán,   Ric - ki,   ric - ki,   ric - ki   ran.

General Translation

This is the way they
saw in San Juan,
making sawdust (aserrín).

Motions

Make a sawing motion forward and back.

Also hold hands with a partner and alternate pushing and pulling with alternate arms.

Bling, Blang

Bling, blang, Ham - mer with my ham - mer.

Zin - go, zan - go, cut - ting with my saw.

Motions

Tap one fist on the other fist during the first line.

With one flat hand held straight, "saw" back and forth on the other hand during the second line.

I Can Hammer

I can ham - mer with one ham - mer,

I can ham - mer with one ham - mer,

I can ham - mer with one ham - mer and

ham - mer and ham - mer all day.

Students are seated on the floor.
During verse one, everyone makes a fist
and taps the beat with a fist on one leg.

Additional Verses & Motions

2. I can hammer with two hammers...
   Move with the beat with two fists tapping
   on legs.

3. I can hammer with three hammers...
   Move with the beat with two fists and
   one foot.

4. I can hammer with four hammers...
   Move with the beat with two fists and
   two feet.

5. I can hammer with five hammers...
   Move with the beat with two fists, two
   feet and your head.

   Older groups sitting in chairs may make
   the fifth motion by alternating between
   standing part way up on one beat and
   sitting down on the next beat.

Johnny Had One Friend

John - ny   had   one friend,   one   friend,   one   friend.

John - ny   had   one   friend,   John - ny   had   two.

Motions

Children tap their legs with one finger until the end when they hold up two fingers.

Verse 2

Johnny had two friends, two friends, two friends.
Johnny had two friends, Johnny had three.

Tap with two fingers, then hold up three.

Continue until children are tapping with all fingers.

Johnny Works with One Hammer

John - ny works with one ham - mer,

One ham - mer, one ham - mer.

John - ny works with one ham - mer,

Then he works with two.

Additional Verses & Motions

Students are seated on the floor. During verse one, each person makes a fist with one hand and taps the beat with a fist on one leg. At the end of the verse, use two fists.

2. Johnny works with two hammers...
Then he works with three.
Tap the beat with two fists on two legs. Add one foot at the end of the verse.

3. Johnny works with three hammers...
Then he works with four.
Tap the beat with both fists and one foot. Add the other foot at the end of the verse.

4. Johnny works with four hammers...
Then he works with five.
Tap the beat with two fists and two feet. Add your head at the end of the verse.

5. Johnny works with five hammers...
Then he's all tired out.
Tap the beat with two fists, two feet, and a nodding head. Stop all motions at the end of the verse.

Older groups sitting in chairs may make the fifth motion by alternating between standing part way up on one beat and sitting down on the next beat.

Kye Kye Kule *Ghanaian*

Leader:

Group:

Kye kye, Ku - le.   Kye kye, Ku - le.

Kye kye Ko - fi nsa.   Kye kye Ko - fi nsa.

Ko - fi nsa lan - ga.   Ko - fi nsa lan - ga.

Ka - ka shi lan - ga.   Ka - ka shi lan - ga.

Kum   a - den - de.   Kum   a - den - de.

All:

Kum   a - den - de.   Hey!

Motions

As the leader introduces each phrase, he or she shows a motion.
The group repeats each phrase and imitates the motion.

Phrase 1: *Pat head four times.*

Phrase 2: *Tap shoulders four times while twisting from side to side.*

Phrase 3: *Tap on waist four times while twisting from side to side.*

Phrase 4: *Tap knees four times.*

Phrase 5: *Touch ankles on "Kum" and waist on "adende."*

Phrase 6: *Leader and group touch ankles and waist again, jump up, and shout, "Hey!"*

Translation

This song's lyrics have no specific meaning.

Mother Goonie Bird

Moth - er Goon - ie Bird___ had sev - en chicks, sev - en chicks had Moth - er Goon - ie Bird,___ And they could - n't walk,___ And they could - n't talk,___ But they all could go like this. "One wing."

Additional Verses & Motions

At the end of verse one as "right foot" is spoken, begin stepping with the beat with the right foot.

2. ..."Left foot"
   Alternate stepping between the right and left foot.

3. ..."Right wing"
   In addition to the previous motions, raise and lower right elbow with the beat.

4. ..."Left wing"
   In addition to the previous motions, raise and lower the left elbow.

5. ..."Now your head"
   In addition to the previous motions, alternate moving head forward and back.

   At the end of the fifth verse say, "Sit down."

My Aunt Came Back

Leader: Group:

Oh, my aunt came back, Oh, my aunt came back,

From Tim - buk - tu, From Tim - buk - tu,

She brought with her, She brought with her,

A wood - en shoe. A wood - en shoe.

(tap foot with the beat)

Additional Verses & Motions

Add a new motion with each verse.

2. Oh, my aunt came back...
   From old Japan...
   She brought with her...
   A waving fan...
   Also fan face with one hand.

3. ...From old Algiers...
   ...A pair of shears...
   Also "snip" using two fingers of the other hand.

4. ...from Guadeloupe...
   ...a hulahoop...
   Also rotate hips.

5. ...from the county fair...
   ...a rocking chair...
   Also rock back and forth.

6. ...from the city zoo...
   ...a nut like YOU!
   Stop motions and point at each other.

My Ship Sailed from China

My ship sailed from Chi - na with a car - go of tea, All

lad - en with pres - ents for you and for me. They

brought me a fan, Just i - mag - ine my bliss, When I

fan my-self dai - ly like this, like this, like this, like this.

Motions

Sit on the floor with legs straight out. Sing the song five times, adding one more motion each time on the last phrase, "Like this, like this, like this, like this."

Continue the motions on the beat as the song is repeated.

1. Fan face with right hand.
2. Fan face with both hands.
3. Fan face with both hands and cross right foot back and forth over left foot.
4. Fan face with both hands and alternate crossing right foot over left foot and left foot over right foot.
5. Fan face with both hands, cross legs back and forth and nod head forward and back.

One Finger, One Thumb

One fin - ger, one thumb, keep mov - ing, keep

mov - ing, keep mov - ing. One

fin - ger, one thumb, keep mov - ing and

chase the flies a - way.

Additional Verses & Motions

Holding up one finger and the thumb of one hand, twist hand back and forth. At "chase the flies away" brush both hands to the side three times.

2. Two fingers, two thumbs, keep moving...

   Hold up finger and thumb of both hands and twist hands back and forth.

3. Two fingers, two thumbs, two arms, keep moving...

   In addition to the previous motions, flap elbows up and down.

4. Two fingers, two thumbs, two arms, two feet, keep moving...

   In addition to the previous motions, lift feet up and down.

5. Two fingers, two thumbs, two arms, two feet, stand up, sit down, keep moving...

   Continue all motions as before and stand up and sit down when those words are sung.

Riding in a Buggy

Rid-ing in a bug-gy Miss   Ma - ry   Jane, Miss

Ma - ry   Jane,   Miss   Ma - ry   Jane.

Rid-ing in a bug-gy Miss   Ma - ry Jane, I'm a

long   ways   from   home.

Motions

1st time:
"We are on our way to a party."
Tap the beat on your legs while singing.

2nd time:
"We must slowly cross through a mud
   puddle."
Tap and sing slower.

3rd time:
"Now we are going to be late for the
   party."
Tap and sing faster.

San Serení   *Puerto Rican*

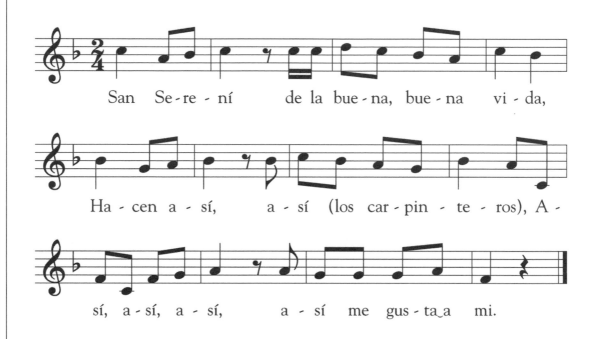

San Se-re-ní   de la bue-na, bue-na   vi-da,

Ha-cen a-sí,   a-sí (los car-pin-te-ros), A-

sí, a-sí, a-sí,   a-sí me gus-ta a mi.

General translation

In San Sereni where life is good,
(carpenters) go like this.

Motions

*Perform motions on the beat as suited to
each verse.*

Verses

1. los carpinteros (carpenters)
2. los zapateros (shoemakers)
3. los campaneros (bell-ringers)
4. las bailarinas (ballerinas)
5. las lavanderas (washerwomen)
6. las pianistas (pianists)
7. los pescadores (fishermen)

The Three Bears

Part 1 Spoken:

Once up-on a time in a nurs-er-y rhyme— There were

three bears,— There were three bears.— A

mom-ma and a pop-pa and a wee bear,— And a

wee bear.— They all went a-walk-in' and a talk-in' in the

woods. A-long came a girl with long curl-y hair.

Part 2 Sung by Goldilocks:

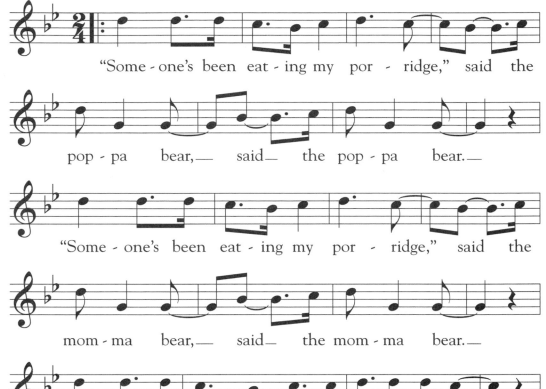

"Some - one's been eat - ing my por - ridge," said the pop - pa bear,— said— the pop - pa bear.—

"Some - one's been eat - ing my por - ridge," said the mom - ma bear,— said— the mom - ma bear.—

"Hey Mom - ma Three Bear," said the lit - tle wee bear,—

"Some - one has eat - en mine up! Yeah!"

Additional Verses

2. Someone's been sitting in my chair....
Someone has broken my chair! Yeah!

3. Someone's been sleeping in my bed....
Someone is sleeping there now! Yeah!

Motions

Maintain the following hand-jive pattern throughout the song:

Tap legs twice, clap hands twice, cross right hand over left hand twice, cross left hand over right hand twice.

Tortillitas *Spanish*

Tor - ti - lli - tas pa - ra ma - má,   tor - ti - lli - tas pa - ra pa - pá,

Las que - ma - di - tas pa - ra ma - má,   las bo - ni - tas pa - ra pa - pá.

Translation

Little tortillas for mama,
Little tortillas for papa,
Crispy ones for mama,
Pretty ones for papa.

Motions

Alternate slapping one hand onto the palm of the other hand on the beat.

Who Stole the Cookie From the Cookie Jar?

Children alternate tapping their legs and clapping their hands.

All: Who stole the cookie from the cookie jar?

Leader: <u>Susan</u> stole the cookie from the cookie jar!

<u>Susan</u>: Who, me?

Leader: Yes, you!

<u>Susan</u>: Couldn't be!

Leader: Then who?

<u>Susan</u>: <u>Jeffery</u> stole the cookie from the cookie jar!

<u>Jeffery</u>: Who, me?

<u>Susan</u>: Yes, you!

Continue until all children have had a turn to speak.

'Twas on a Monday Morning

'Twas on a Mon - day morn - ing, When I be - held my

dar - ling, She looked so neat and charm - ing, In

ev - 'ry high de - gree.— She looked so neat and

nim - ble - O, A - wash - ing of her lin - en - O.

Dash - ing a - way with the smooth - ing iron,

Dash - ing a - way with the smooth - ing iron, She

stole my heart— a - way.———

Additional Verses & Motions

2. ...Tuesday...A-starching of...
3. ...Wednesday...A-hanging out...
4. ...Thursday...A-ironing of...
5. ...Friday...A-folding of...

6. ...Saturday...A-airing of...
7. ...Sunday...A-wearing of...

Act out the motions of each verse with the beat of the song.

Head and Shoulders, Baby

Head and shoulders, baby,
*Tap head and shoulders with both hands.
Then cross arms and touch opposite shoulders.*
One,
Tap legs and clap hands once.
Two,
Tap legs and clap hands once.
Three,
Tap legs once.
Head and shoulders, baby,
Same motions as before.
One, two, three,
Tap legs, clap hands, tap legs, clap hands, tap legs.
Head and shoulders,
Tap head then shoulders.
Head and shoulders,
Tap head then shoulders.
Head and shoulders, baby,
Tap head and shoulders. Then cross arms and touch opposite shoulders.
One, two, three.
Tap legs, clap hands, tap legs, clap hands, tap legs.

Make up additional verses with other body parts, such as:

Knees and ankles, baby...
or
Cheeks and chin, baby...

My Name Is Joe

Hi! My name is Joe.
I have a wife and three kids,
And I work in a button factory.
One day my boss said,
"Joe, are you busy?"
I said, "No."
He said,
"Turn the button with your right hand."
Pretend to hold an object with the right hand and turn it back and forth with the beat while repeating the rhyme.

2. ..."Turn the button with your left hand."
Both hands turn "buttons."

3. ..."Turn the button with your right elbow."
Both hands turn "buttons" while raising and lowering right elbow.

4. ..."Turn the button with your left elbow."
Both hands turn "buttons" while raising and lowering both elbows.

5. ..."Turn the button with your right foot."
Continue previous motions while tapping right foot out and in pivoting on the heel.

6. ..."Turn the button with your left foot."
Continue previous motions while tapping both feet out and in pivoting on heels.

7. ..."Turn the button with your head."
Continue previous motions while nodding head with the beat. This verse ends:
"Joe, are you busy?"
I said, "YES!"
At the end, stop all motions and shake fists in the air in frustration.

Wash the Dishes

Wash the dishes, dry the dishes,

Two children hold hands and swing arms back and forth.

Turn the dishes over.
Still holding hands, turn under so children are standing back to back.

Repeat rhyme and turn under again so children are facing each other.

We're Gonna Go on a Bear Hunt

Children repeat each line after the leader.

We're gonna go on a bear hunt.
Alternately tap hands on legs.
All right let's go.

Oh look,
I see a wheat field.
Can't go over it.
Reach up high.
Can't go under it.
Squat very low to the floor.
Can't go around it.
Sway to one side then the other.
We'll have to go through it.
Swish, swish, swish, swish, swish, swish, swish, swish.
Rub hands together making a swishing sound.

Oh look,
I see a tree.
Can't go over it.
Reach up high.
Can't go under it.
Squat very low to the floor.
Can't go around it.
Sway to one side then the other.
We'll have to climb up it.
Climb, climb, climb, climb, climb, climb, climb, climb.
Alternate hands reaching in climbing motion.

Oh look,
I see a swamp.
Can't go over it.
Reach up high.
Can't go under it.
Squat very low to the floor.
Can't go around it.
Sway to one side then the other.
We'll have to swim through it.
Swim, swim, swim, swim, swim, swim, swim, swim.
Alternate hands making a swimming motion.

Oh look,
I see a bridge.
Can't go over it.
Reach up high.
Can't go under it.
Squat very low to the floor.
Can't go around it.
Sway to one side then the other.
We'll have to cross it.
Stomp, stomp, stomp, stomp, stomp, stomp, stomp, stomp.
Pound fists on floor, alternating hands.

Oh look,
I see a cave.
Can't go over it.
Reach up high.
Can't go under it.
Squat very low to the floor.
Can't go around it.
Sway to one side then the other.
We'll have to go in it.
Tip-toe, tip-toe, tip-toe, tip-toe.
It's dark in here.
Whoooo.
Whoooo.
I feel something soft,
And warm,
And furry,
It's a bear!
Do all previous motions very fast in reverse order; tip-toe, stomp, stomp, swim, swim, climb, climb, swish, swish, tap hands on thighs and wipe forehead with hand.
Whew! We found the bear!

Zodio

This song is sung with a swing.

Partners hold both hands and make a swing motion.

Here we go Zo - di - o, zo - di - o, zo - di - o,

Here we go zo - di - o all night long.

With hands released step back four steps.

Step back Sal - ly, Sal - ly, Sal - ly.

Step toward partner four steps.

Step back Sal - ly all night long. I

With hands on hips dip left shoulder in and out.

went to the al - ley, and what did I see? A

big fat man from Ten - nes - see.

Bet - cha five dol - lars I can beat that man,

Bet - cha five dol - lars I can beat that man. To the

With hands on hips jump in once, jump out once, jump left once, jump right once, jump to the center; repeat.

front, to the back, to the side, side, side,— To the

front, to the back, to the side, side, side,— I

Shake finger.

went to the doc - tor. The doc - tor said,

Hold head and rock head on beat, hands on hips and sway hips on beat.

"Ooh, ah, I got a pain in my head,
Ooh, ah, I got a pain in my side.

Point to toe on the beat.

Ooh, ah, I got a pain in my toe,"— To the

With hands on hips jump in once, jump out once, jump left once, jump right once, jump to the center; repeat.

front, to the back, to the side, side, side,— To the

front, to the back, to the side, side, side.—

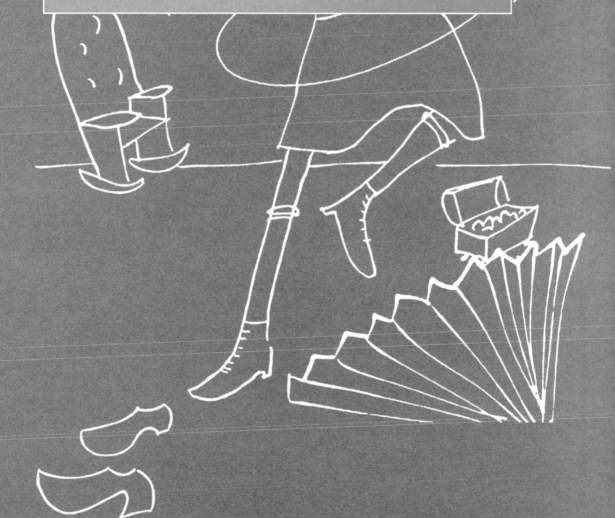

STATIONARY
CIRCLES

Circle 'Round the Zero

Cir-cle 'round the ze-ro.   Find your lov-in' ze-ro.

Back,   back,   ze-ro.   Side,   side,   ze-ro.

Front,   front,   ze-ro.   Tap your lov-in'   ze-ro.

Motions

The group stands in a circle and taps the beat on their legs while Child A walks around the outside of the circle.

back, back
  Child A stands back-to-back with one of the children in the circle, Child B.

side, side
  Child A stands side-by-side with Child B.

front, front
  Child A moves inside the circle to face Child B.

tap your lovin'
  Child A taps the shoulders of Child B.

The game repeats with Child A returning to the circle and Child B walking around the outside of the circle.

Draw Me a Bucket of Water

Draw me a buck-et of wa - ter,

for my la - dy's daugh - ter, There's

one on the bush and two in the bush, and

num - ber (one) pops un - der.

Motions

Divide students into groups of four. Each group of four forms a square. Each person holds hands with the person across from them. The first couple (Couple A) links hands above those of the second couple (Couple B). Each couple moves hands back and forth in a chugging motion. During the last phrase, one couple lifts their arms over and around one of the persons in the other couple as follows:

Verse 1

number one pops under
Couple A lifts their arms over and around one of the persons in Couple B.

Verse 2

number two pops under
Couple A lifts their arms over and around the other person in Couple B.

Verse 3

number three pops under
Couple B lifts their arms over and around one of the persons in Couple A.

Verse 4

number four pops under
Couple B lifts their arms over and around the other person in Couple A.

During the fifth repetition, each foursome joins hands, leans back, and turns quickly in a circle. The song ends with "everyone pops under," and everyone lets go of each other's hands.

Doctor Knickerbocker I

Doc-tor Knick-er-bock-er, Knick-er-bock-er, num-ber nine.— Oh, s/he fell down and— broke his/her spine.— Now, let's get the rhy-thm of the hands. *(clap, clap)* Now, we've got the rhy-thm of the hands. *(clap, clap)* Now, let's get the rhy-thm of the feet. *(stamp, stamp)* Now, we've got the rhy-thm of the feet. *(stamp, stamp)* Now let's get the rhy-thm of the num-ber nine!— 1 2 3 4 5 6 7 8 9!

Motions to Doctor Knickerbocker I

The group stands in a circle with one person in the center. Everyone in the circle claps their hands on the second beat of each measure. The person in the center sings the solos and makes up various motions. Everyone in the circle echoes and imitates the motions. At the end, everyone counts to nine while the one in the center covers his or her eyes and turns around while pointing, stopping on the number nine. Whoever is being pointed to becomes the next person in the center.

Doctor Knickerbocker II

Children stand in a circle

Doc-tor

(Rapidly pat hands on legs)

Knickerbocker, Knickerbocker,
number nine,

Alternately clap own hands and reach out in both directions to clap hands of those on each side. Continue this pattern.

You can keep a rhythm most any old time.

Now, let's put the rhythm in your feet.

Two stomps.

Now let's put the rhythm on your legs.

Tap legs two times.

Now let's put the rhythm in our hands.

Clap hands two times.

Now let's put the rhythm on our heads.

Tap head two times.

Start the game slowly and increase speed with each repetition.

Here Comes Missis Macaroni

Here comes Mis-sis Mac-a-ro-ni, Rid-ing on her

milk white po-ny, Here she comes with all her mon-ey,

Mis-sis Mac-a-ro-ni. Hong Kong, Hong Kong,

Su-zi-an-na, Hong Kong, Hong Kong, Su-zi-an-na,

Hong Kong, Hong Kong, Su-zi-an-na,

Mis-sis Mac-a-ro-ni.

Motions

The group stands in a circle with one child in the center. During the first two phrases, the circle walks in one direction while "Mr./Mrs. Macaroni" walks inside the circle in the opposite direction. During the third phrase, the children in the circle stop and clap their hands while Mr./Mrs. Macaroni chooses someone to hold hands with and promenade around the inside of the circle. At the end of the song, the original Mr./Mrs. Macaroni returns to the circle and the selected partner becomes the new Mr./Mrs. Macaroni.

Little Johnny Brown

All:
Lit - tle John - ny Brown, lay your com - fort down,

Lit - tle John - ny Brown, lay your com - fort down.

Leader:
Fold down your cor - ner, John - ny Brown,

Fold down your cor - ner, John - ny Brown.

Fold down your cor - ner, John - ny Brown,

Fold down your cor - ner, John - ny Brown.

Group:

Motions

The group stands in a circle clapping hands on the off beats. During the first two phrases, one child walks around the inside of the circle carrying a handkerchief. During the call and response, the child in the center sets the kerchief down in front of a selected child and sings the leader part, asking him or her to fold the corners into the center of the kerchief. At the end of the song, the selected child picks up the kerchief and the game repeats from the beginning.

Old Obidiah

1. Old   Ob - i - di - ah   jumped   in the   fire   and the

2. Fire   was   hot   so he   jumped   in the   pot   and the
3. Pot   was   black   so he   jumped   in the   crack   and the
4. Crack   was   high   so he   jumped   in the   sky   and the
5. Sky   was   blue   so he   jumped   in the   canoe   and the
6. Canoe   was shallow   so he   jumped   in the   tallow   and the
7. Tallow   was   soft   so he   jumped   in the   loft   and the
8. Loft   was   rotten   so he   jumped   in the   cotton   and the
9. Cotton   was   white   so he

slept   all   night.

Motions

*Everyone stands in a circle, alternately
clapping their hands and then reaching to
both sides and clapping the hands of the
children on both sides. The group
maintains this clapping pattern while
adding the jumps; the group jumps once
into the center (on the word "jumped")
and jumps out two beats later.*

Pizza, Pizza

Group:

(Ja - son) has a girl friend, Piz - za, piz - za, dad-dy - o,

Leader: 3

Group:

How do you know it? Piz - za, piz - za, dad-dy - o,

'Cause she told me. Piz - za, piz - za, dad-dy - o,

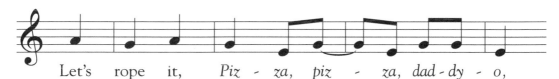

Let's rope it, Piz - za, piz - za, dad-dy - o,

Let's (throw it), Piz - za, piz - za, dad-dy - o,

Leader:

Let's end it.

Motions

The group stands in a circle with one child in the center.

Motions for "Pizza, pizza, daddy-o" are performed by all as follows:

1. Jump and land with feet apart.
2. Jump and land with right foot crossed over left foot.
3. Jump and land with feet apart.
4. Jump and land with left foot crossed in front of right foot.
5. Jump and land with feet together.

The child in the center sings and performs as many different motions as he or she wishes. When finished, he or she covers his or her eyes, turns around pointing, and sings, "Let's end it." The leader stops turning and the child who is being pointed to becomes the next leader.

Ali Baba

Leader chants the following phrase while performing some motion with the beat.

Ali Baba and the forty thieves.

Group repeats the phrase and the motions shown by the leader. The leader continues demonstrating different motions, each repeated by the group.

Later: The leader performs some motion while speaking the phrase. While the group is repeating the phrase with those motions, the leader shows the next motion. While the children are performing the second motion, the leader shows the third motion etc.

Still Later: Children sit in a circle. The leader performs some motion while speaking the phrase. The next child in the circle repeats that motion while the leader shows the second motion. As the leader shows the third motion, the next child is performing the second motion and the child next to him or her is performing the first motion. The passing of the motion is continued until all children are performing different motions with the beat concurrently.

Buzz

Everyone sits in a circle and taps the beat on their legs throughout the game. No one is allowed to say any number that contains the number seven (seven, seventeen, twenty-seven etc.) or any multiple of seven (fourteen, twenty-one, etc.) Begin with the first person saying "one." The next says "two." And so on until the num-

ber seven. That child should say, "Buzz." (Buzz-Buzz for seventy-seven!) If a child says "buzz" at the wrong time or forgets to say "buzz" when they should, they are out. Continue until one child is left.

Variation 1

Try the game with other numbers and multiples of that number.

Variation 2

Try saying "buzz" for numbers involving seven and "fizz" for numbers involving the number five (or another number).

Jigama, Jigama

Jigama, jigama, honey cup.
How many fingers do I hold up?

One child taps the beat on the back of another child while holding up one to five fingers.

Three she said and ____ it was,
Jigama, jigama, honey cup.

If the child guesses correctly it is his or her turn to tap on the other child's back. If not, the same child repeats the tapping.

The Minister's Cat

The minister's cat is a ____ cat.

Children sit in a circle tapping on their legs. One at a time each child chants the following phrase and inserts some word to describe the cat. Example: "The minister's cat is a fluffy cat." Each child should start immediately after the preceding child without missing a beat. No child can use the same word a previous child has used.

With older children try the following variations:

Variation 1

Each child makes up a word to describe the cat that begins with the letter "A." When a child is stumped move to the next letter in the alphabet. Now the stumped child and all subsequent children speak the phrase inserting a word that begins with the letter "B." Each time a child is stumped move to the next letter.

Variation 2

Each child makes up a word beginning with the next letter in the alphabet.

Variation 3

Use the alphabet backwards. Each child makes up a word beginning with the letter before the previous letter.

Variation 4

Each child makes up a word that begins with the last letter of the word made up by the previous child.

Neighbor, Neighbor

Children sit in a circle.

Neighbor, neighbor how art thee?
Spoken by one child while performing some motion on the beat.

Very fine as you can see.
Spoken by the child next to him as he imitates that motion.

How's thy neighbor next to thee?
Spoken by the first child repeating the original motion.

I don't know, but I'll go see.
Spoken by the second child as he again imitates the motion.

The second child starts the rhyme over, selecting a new motion for child number three to imitate. Continue the game until all children have had a turn.

Who's the Leader?

One child leaves the room.

With everyone standing in a circle, one is selected to be the leader. The leader performs some motion with the beat. The group will do whatever the leader does. The single child returns and stands in the center of the circle and tries to guess who the leader is. When the person in the center is not looking, the leader changes his or her motion. All try to switch to the leader's motion immediately and try not to look at the leader. The child in the center gets three guesses to discover "who the leader is."

This can be done with or without recorded music playing.

Nievie, Nievie

Nievie, nievie, nick, nack,
Which one will you tic-tac?
Tac one, tac two,
Tac the best of them for you.
I'll tac this, I'll tac that.
I'll tac nievie nick-nack!

A small group of children stand in a circle. The first child puts one hand into the center with palm down. Maintaining the beat of the poem, the next child places his or her hand on top of the first hand. Children continue around the circle placing their hands on top. The second time around the circle each child places his or her other hand on the pile. Each subsequent time around the circle each child removes his or her hand from the bottom of the pile and places it on top of the pile. Gradually increase the speed.

Tweedle, Tweedle

Children sit in a circle and alternate between tapping the beat on their legs with and without arms crossed while the following dialogue travels around to the left:

Leader: Have you seen my flute?
Person 1: Does it toot?
Leader: It toots.
Person 1: How does it toot?
Leader: Tweedle, tweedle, toot!
Person 1: Have you seen his flute?
Person 2: Does it toot?
Person 1: It toots.

Person 2: How does it toot?
Leader: Tweedle, tweedle, toot!
Person 2: Have you seen his flute?
Person 3: Does it toot?
Person 2: It toots.
Person 3: How does it toot?
Leader: Tweedle, tweedle, toot!
Person 3: Have you seen his flute?
Person 4: Does it toot?
Person 3: It toots.
    Etc...

Way Down Yonder

Leader:

Group:

Way   down   yon - der,   Some - times,

Be - low   the   log,   Some - times,

Wild__ geese   are   holl - 'rin',   Some - times,

Gan - ders   trot,   Some - times,

Bull - frog   mar - ry,   Some - times,

His   moth - er - in - law.   Some - times,

Now,   let's   get   on   board,—   Some - times,

I'm   goin'   to   ball   that   jack,   Some - times,

Un - til my hon - ey comes back, Some - times,

I want to rear back, Jack, Some - times,

And get a hump in my back, Some - times,

I'm goin' o - ver here, Some - times,

Goin' to get my pal. Some - times.___

Motions

One child walks around the inside of the circle. Those in the circle alternate between clapping their own hands and reaching out to both sides to clap the hands with both sides simultaneously. At "now let's get on board," the one in the middle stands in front of one child. The child in the middle performs some motion, and the child facing him or her imitates the motion.

At "I want to rear back Jack," the two children hold hands and spin around in the center of the circle while leaning back. At "I'm goin' over here," the original child takes the place of the chosen child and the game repeats with the new child in the center of the circle.

Wee Melody Man

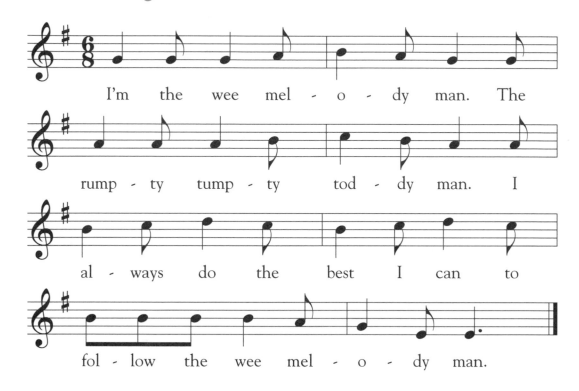

I'm the wee mel - o - dy man. The
rump - ty tump - ty tod - dy man. I
al - ways do the best I can to
fol - low the wee mel - o - dy man.

Motions

Everyone sits in a circle and one child is designated to be the first leader. During the first runthrough, everyone pretends to play various instruments moving with the beat of the song. During the second runthrough, the leader imitates one of the other children. The child who is being imitated must discover before the end of the song that the leader is performing his or her motion and switch to the leader's previous motion. If he or she is successful, he or she becomes the next leader. If not, the current leader may continue for another turn.

Wishy Washy

Oh, we are two sail-ors late-ly come from sea, And if you want an-oth-er one, come a-long with me. Oh, wish-y wash-y, wish-y wash-y, wish-y wash-y wee, And if you want an-oth-er one, come a-long with me.

Motions

The group stands in a circle with two children in the center. During the first two phrases, those two children swing each other around by one arm. During the last two phrases, the two in the center both choose partners from the circle. These two couples put their hands on each other's shoulders and kick their legs in opposite directions while the others in the circle clap their hands. At the end of the song, the original two children return to the circle, the two new children remain in the center and the game repeats.

Passing Objects

Stick, Stick

With Child A in the center, students sit cross legged, with knees touching, and form a circle. The left hand forms a "cup" shape (palm up) and is placed on the right knee of the person to the left (each person has someone else's left hand on their right knee). The right hand is made into a clenched position (as though hiding something). One person starts with a twig small enough to be concealed in their right hand. Child A must know where the stick is starting.

The players should practice the motions before the game begins. They all start with their right hand in the cupped hand of the player whose hand is on their right knee. At the same time everyone moves their right hand into their own left hand, then back to the other hand, then back to their own hand. The stick is passed from one player to the next, but must be concealed to the best of their abilities (especially during the actual passing of the stick). After the poem is spoken once, Child A can begin to guess who has the stick. The circle repeats the poem until Child A guesses

who has the stick. At that point, those two players switch places. Half the fun is trying to conceal the stick—the other half is pretending you have it when you really don't!

The poem is as follows. The group's hands go from side to side at each line break.

Stick,
Stick.
How I
Wonder,
From one
hand in-
to the
other.
Is it
fair?
Is it
fair? To
keep poor
(name of player in center)
sitting
there?

Cup, Stick & Stone Passing

Patterns in 2

Using only right hand:
1. *Pick up object.*
2. *Set down to the right.*

Patterns in 3

Using only right hand:
1. *Pick up object.*
2. *Touch object to the floor.*
3. *Set down to the right.*

Patterns in 4

Using only right hand:
1. *Pick up object.*
2. *Touch object to the floor.*
3. *Lift object above head.*
4. *Set down to the right.*

Patterns in 5

Using only right hand:
1. *Pick up object.*
2. *Touch object to the floor.*
3. *Lift object above head.*
4. *Touch object to the floor.*
5. *Set down to the right.*

The Wonder Ball

The wonder ball goes 'round and 'round,
To pass it quickly, you are bound.
If you're the one to hold it last,
Then for you the game is past!

*The group forms a circle and passes a ball
around the circle on the beat. The one
holding the ball on the word "past" is out.*

This Is a Pencil

*The leader of the game introduces all the
objects that will be used for the game.
There must be one object for each player.
Everyone must look at the person to whom
he or she is speaking.*

Person 1: This is a pencil.
(*Person 1 picks up the pencil and sets it
down in front of the person to his/her right*)
Person 2: A what?
Person 1: A pencil.
Person 2: A what?
Person 1: A pencil.
Person 2: Oh, a pencil.

*This is repeated with Person 2 picking up
the pencil and setting it down in front of
Person 3 to his or her right. At the same
time, Person 2 picks up the pencil, Person
1 introduces a new object and says, "This
is a _____." Person 2 will now look at
Person 1 while asking the questions and on
the next beat look at Person 3 answering
the question. Continue until all persons
are passing objects.*

Al Citron *Mexican*

Al ci - tron de un fan - dan - go, San - go,

San - go Sa - ba - ré.   Sa - ba - ré de

la ron - de - la Con su tri - ki, tri - ki - trón.

Motions

Everyone sits in a circle with legs crossed and knees almost touching. Each child has an object in front of him or her such as a cup, a pebble, or a pencil. Everyone picks up the object on the upbeat and sets the object down in front of the person to their right on the downbeat of every measure. While "triki, trikitrón" is sung, everybody touches the object to the right, the object to the left, and sets his or her object down in front of the person on the right.

Translation

Though this song's lyrics have no specific meaning, some of the words have translations. A *citron* is a type of fruit, and a *fandango* is a type of dance.

I Give You a Cat

Motions

The group sits in a circle with legs crossed and knees almost touching. The circle passes around an object (a "cat") going clockwise. As each person passes the object, he or she taps the floor in front of the next person, brings the object back to him or herself, taps the floor in front of him or herself with the object, and finally gives the object to the next person. After the group has been passing one object around the circle, the group can introduce another object (a "dog") around the circle, passing in the opposite direction.

I Pass the Shoe

I pass the shoe from me to you, to you. I

pass the shoe and this is what I do.

Motions

The group sits in a circle with legs crossed and knees almost touching. With the right hand, have children tap the beat on the floor, first in front of themselves and then in front of the person sitting to the right of them while chanting, "In front, to the right, in front, to the right." Once this motion is secure, have the group continue the tapping motion while a shoe (or some other object) is passed around on the beat.

When the object lands in front of a child, his/her hand should land on it with the words "In front" and he or she should pass it to the right with the words "to the right." Once the group is comfortable passing on the beat, everyone can try singing the song while also tapping and passing.

With advanced groups, try passing as many objects as there are children, so that all children are passing objects continuously through the song.

Obwisana *Ghanaian*

Ob - wi - sa - na   sa - na-na,   Ob - wi - sa - na - sa.

Ob - wi - sa - na   sa - na-na,   Ob - wi - sa - na - sa.

Motions

The group sits on the floor in a circle with their legs crossed and knees nearly touching. Each person has a small object (rock) in front of him or her. With his or her right hand, each child picks up the object and sets it down in front of the person on the right. The object should be set down at the beginning of each measure.

Translation

I just hurt my finger on a rock, grandma.

Where, Oh, Where

Leader:

Where, oh, where, Where, oh, where,

The li - on, The li - on,

One and one and one and one. One and one and one and one.

Pass the peb - ble down, Pass the peb - ble down.

Group:

Motions

Everyone sits in a circle with their legs crossed and their knees almost touching. Each person begins with a pebble in front of him or her and performs the following motions: 1) Pick up the pebble with the right hand. 2) Pass the pebble from the right hand to the left hand. 3) Set the pebble down in front of the person sitting to the left (the motions should be practiced ahead of time). This three-beat motion is especially fun with the two beat meter of the song.

Passing the Beat

Checkerberry

Checkerberry,
Checkerberry,
Checkerberry on.

The group stands in a circle. Each person makes up a motion to perform on the beat while chanting "Checkerberry, Checkerberry, Checkerberry on." While performing their motions, each person looks at the motion performed on the right. As the chant is repeated, each child performs the motion from the person on his or her right. Continue until each child is performing his or her original motion.

Down on the Banks of the Hanky Panky

Down on the banks of the Hanky Panky
Where the bullfrogs jump from bank
   to banky,
With a hip-hop, flippity-flop.
One, two, three, four, five – you're out!

Everyone stands in a circle with palms up and right hand resting in the left hand of the person to the right. One at a time, each person lifts his right hand and claps onto the right hand of the person on his or her left. Continue through the poem until the last line and then speed up and clap a hand with each number. The person whose hand is clapped on the word "out" leaves the game.

Take It

This activity is done with recorded music appropriate for keeping a steady beat, such as those found on the CD First Steps in Classical Music: Keeping the Beat. Students stand in a circle. Child A begins by tapping a steady beat and everyone imitates that motion. Child A then calls on Child B who changes the motion while continuing to maintain a steady beat. All other students switch to the new motion without missing a beat. Continue until all students have had an opportunity to "take it."

A Quackadilioso

A quack-a-dil-i-o-so quack, quack, quack;—

Señ - or-i - ta, ri-ta, ri-ta, ri - ra, ri -

ra,—— Ve - lor,—— ve - lor, ve-lor, ve-lor ve-lor!

1, 2, 3, 4!

Motions

The group sits in a circle. Everyone places their left hands out to the left with palms up. Everyone rests their right hands (palms up) onto the left palm of the person to their right. Keeping the beat, the first person taps his or her right hand onto the palm of the right hand of the person to his or her left. The next person does the same and so on as the beat motion travels around the circle. The person who is tapped on "4" is out. The game continues until only one person is left.

BEATS

in Groups of 2 & 3

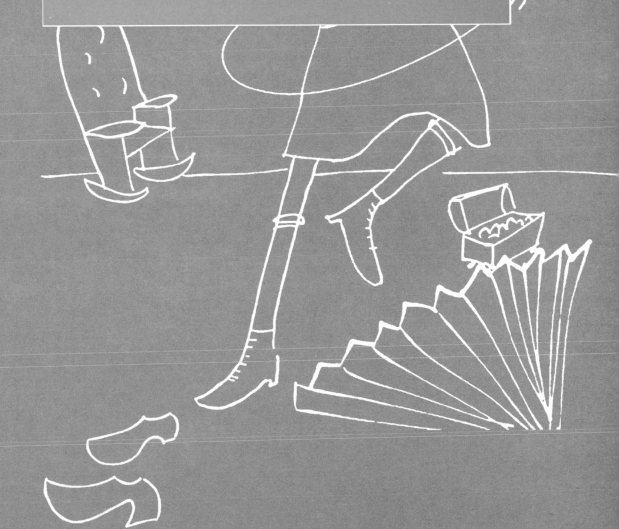

Introduction

Following are some of the many possible beat motions that might be performed with the beat in 2s or 3s. It may be helpful to chant a descriptive word while performing a motion with the beat.

Stamp

Nod your head "yes"

Chug (swing elbows)

Swing arms forward and back

Swing a leg

Row a boat

Swim

Paddle a canoe

Sway

Shake hands

Bend

Stretch any body part in any
    direction

Snap fingers

Twist

Slide

Skate

Push

Pull

Hit

Shrink

Squeeze
Lunge
Stalk
Creep
Lift
Punch
Smack Lips
Knock knees
Click tongues
Tug ears
Hammer fists "one-potato style"
Swing arms bending low
Shrug shoulders
Point one toe then the other
Tap any part of your body
Clap
Step
Shake head "no"
Jump with both feet
Hop on one foot
Blink
Bounce from your knees while
 standing
Bounce from your knees while
 kneeling
Swing hips from side to side
Tiptoe
Tap the floor
Flap hands
Wink
Wave
Pat

Shake any body part
Run
Shuffle
March
Knock
Punch the air with alternating arms
Wash the window
"Shoo" with hands
Cross hands in front
Lift a knee
Swing a leg
Clap with two fingers
Conduct in patterns 2 or 3
Alternate tapping legs and clapping
 hands

Moving with a Prop

Following are some of the many possible props to hold while performing steady beat motions.

Paper plates
Balloons
Rhythm sticks
Feather dusters
Ribbons
Streamers taped to pencils
Scarves
Styrofoam or paper cups
Small flags

Beats in 2

The following songs and rhymes offer very clear feelings of beats in groups of two. Perform various beat motions in groups of two "here" and two "there" while performing these songs and rhymes.

All the Birds

All the birds that I could mention,
Meet to hold a big convention!
How they cluster, how they muster,
How they flitter, flutter, fluster!
Now they dart with gleaming feather,
Now they cuddle all together!

-Aristophanes

All Fools Day

The first of April some do say
Is set apart for All Fools Day.
But why the people call it so
Not I nor they themselves do know.
But on this day are people sent
On purpose for pure merriment.

-Poor Robin's Almanac

Betty Botter

Betty Botter bought some butter,
"But," she said, "this butter's bitter.
If I put it in my batter,
It will make my batter bitter.
But a bit of better butter,
That would make my batter better."
So she bought a bit of butter
Better than her bitter butter.
And she put it in her batter,
And the batter was not bitter.
So 'twas better Betty Botter
Bought a bit of better butter.

Cinderella

Cinderella dressed in yellow
Went upstairs to kiss a fellow.

Doctor Fell

I do not like thee, Doctor Fell,
The reason why I cannot tell.
But this I know and know full well,
I do not like thee, Doctor Fell.

Ducky Duddles

Ducky Duddles
Loves the puddles.
How he waddles
As he paddles
In the puddles;
Ducky Duddles!

Hearts

Hearts, like doors will open with ease
To very, very little keys.
And don't forget that two of these
Are "I thank you," and "If you
please."

Jerry Hall

Jerry Hall,
He is so small.
A rat could eat him,
Hat and all.

A Kite

I often sit and wish that I
Could be a kite up in the sky,
And ride upon the breeze and go
Whichever way I choose to blow.

Little Guinea Pig

There was a little guinea pig
Who, being little, was not big.
He always walked upon his feet
And never fasted when he eat.

When from a place he ran away,
He never at that place did stay.
And while he ran as I am told,
He ne'er stood still for young or old.

One day, as I am certified,
He took a whim and fairly died.
And as I'm told by men of sense,
He never has been living since!

A Man of Words

A man of words and not of deeds
Is like a garden full of weeds.
And when the weeds begin to grow,
It's like a garden full of snow.
And when the snow begins to fall,
It's like a bird upon a wall.
And when the bird away does fly,
It's like an eagle in the sky.
And when the sky begins to roar,
It's like a lion at the door;
And when the door begins to crack,
It's like a stick across your back.
And when your back begins to smart,
It's like a penknife in your heart;
And when your heart begins to bleed
You're dead and dead is dead indeed.

Money Spent

When land is gone and money spent
Then learning is most excellent.

Peter Pumpkin Eater

Peter, Peter, pumpkin eater,
Had a wife and couldn't keep her.
Put her in a pumpkin shell
And there he kept her very well.

St. Dunstan

St. Dunstan, as the story goes,
Once pulled the devil by his nose,
With red-hot tongs, which made
    him roar
That could be heard ten miles or
    more.

St. Paul's Steeple

On St. Paul's steeple stands a tree
As full of apples as may be.
The little boys of London town
They run with hooks to pull them
    down,
And then they run from hedge to
    hedge
Until they come to London Bridge.

A Parrot

Clothed in yellow, red, and green,
I prate before the king and queen.
Of neither house nor land possessed,
By lords and knights I am caressed.
(A parrot)

Shoe Our Pony

O will you shoe our pony, pray?
To Basel we would ride away!
What shall he carry on his back?
A cruller in a paper sack,
A little cheese, some curds, and whey,
And we'll come back tomorrow day!

Una Vieja   *Spanish*

Una vieja pisa un gato,
Con la punta del zapato.
Pobre vieja, pobre gato,
Pobre punta de zapato.

Wise Old Owl

A wise old owl sat in an oak;
The more he heard the less he spoke.
The less he spoke, the more he heard.
Why aren't we all like that old bird!

I Dropped My Dolly

I dropped my dol - ly in the dirt. I
asked my dol - ly if it hurt, And all my dol - ly
had to say was, "Waa waa waa waa waa."

King William

King Wil - liam was King James - 's son, And
he the roy - al race did run. He
wore a star up - on his breast. It
point - ed east; it point - ed west.

Minka

From the Vol-ga I was rid-ing, On my great horse

no-bly strid-ing, When I saw a shad-ow hid-ing,

Min-ka, charm-ing Min-ka. Min-ka, Min-ka

I have spied thee, Do not in the for-est hide thee,

On my great horse I will ride thee, Min-ka, charm-ing Min-ka.

Old Aunt Kate

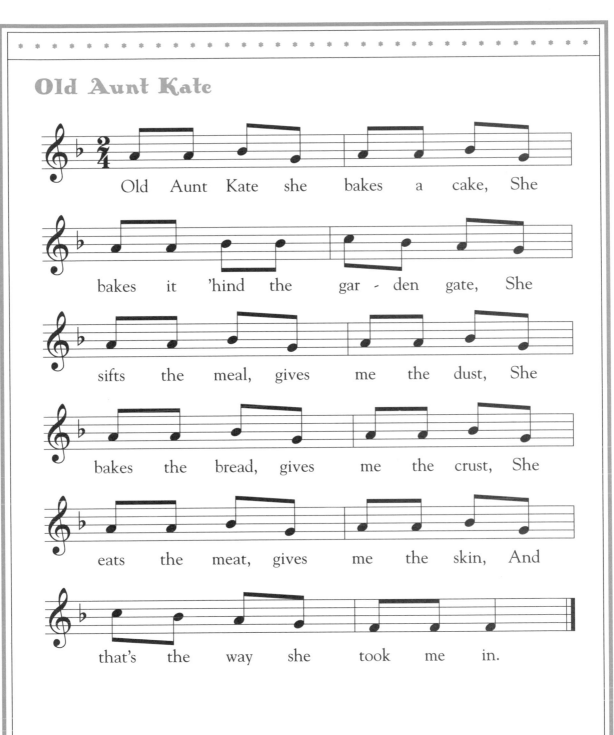

Old Aunt Kate she bakes a cake, She

bakes it 'hind the gar - den gate, She

sifts the meal, gives me the dust, She

bakes the bread, gives me the crust, She

eats the meat, gives me the skin, And

that's the way she took me in.

Beats in 3

The following songs and rhymes offer very clear feelings of beats in groups of three. Perform various beat motions in groups of three "here" and three "there" while performing these songs and rhymes.

"Baroque and Blue"

Suite for Flute
("Baroque and Blue")
by Claude Bolling

Students listen to the recording and perform the beats in groups of two or three. Place one group "here" and one group "there." Students should discover that the music alternates between moving in two and moving in three.

Moses Supposes

Moses supposes his toeses are roses
But Moses supposes erroneously.
For nobody's toeses are posies of roses
As Moses supposes his toeses to be.

Old Mother Goose

Old Mother Goose
When she wanted to wander,
Would ride through the air
On a very fine gander.

Sing at the Table

Sing at the table or whistle in bed,
You'll shake hands with the devil
before you are dead!

Bryan O'Lin

Bryan O'Lin had no breeches to wear
So he bought him a sheepskin and
    made him a pair,
With the shiny side out and the
    wooly side in.
"Well, Ah ha! That is warm!" said
Ole Bryan O'Lin.

Terence McDiddler

Terence McDiddler,
The three-stringed fiddler
Can charm, if he please
All the fish in the seas.

A Well

As round as an apple,
As deep as a cup,
And yet all the king's horses
Can not pull it up.

(A well)

Blow the Wind

Blow the wind south - er - ly, south - er - ly, south - er - ly,

Blow the wind o - ver the sea.

Cockles and Mussels

In Dub - lin's fair cit - y where girls are so pret - ty, I

first set my eyes on sweet Mol - ly Ma - lone. As she

wheeled her wheel - bar - row through streets broad and nar - row, cryin',

"Cock - les and mus - sels, a - live, a - live - o."

Verse 2

She was a fish monger, and sure 'twas
no wonder,
For so was her father and mother
before,
As they wheeled their wheelbarrows
through streets broad and narrow,
Cryin', "Cockles and mussels, alive,
alive-o."

Verse 3

She died of a fever and no one could
save her,
And that was the end of sweet Molly
Malone.
Now her ghost wheels her 'barrow
through streets broad and narrow,
Cryin', "Cockles and mussels, alive,
alive-o."

Oh, Dear

Oh, dear, what can the mat - ter be?

Dear, dear, what can the mat - ter be?

Oh, dear, what can the mat - ter be?

Fine

John - ny's so long at the fair.

He pro-mised to buy me a trin-ket to please me, And

then for a kiss, O he vowed he would tease me, He

D.C. al Fine

prom - ised to bring me a bunch of blue rib - bons to

tie up my bon - ny brown hair.

Schumann Lullaby Op. 124, No. 6

the book of songs & rhymes with beat motions

Washer Woman

Get a wom-an, a wom-an, a good wash-er wom-an, a

wom-an, a wom-an, a good wash-er wom-an, a

wom-an, a wom-an, a good wash-er wom-an, You'll

nev - er re - gret it, you'll nev - er de - spair.

Optional Lyrics

Oh, Mactavish is dead and his
  brother don't know it,
His brother is dead and Mactavish
  don't know it.
They're both of them dead and
  they're in the same bed
And so neither one knows that the
  other is dead.

Yo, Mamana, Yo (Oh, Mama, Oh) *Mozambique*

Yo, ma - ma - na, yo, Yo, ma - ma - na,

yo, Un - ga fam - ba u - ni si - ya.

U - ni si - ye - la vusi - wa - na.

Motions

Gently pat the first beat of each measure on the lap with two fingers. Then pat beats two and three into the palm of the other hand with two fingers.

Another option is to have children form a circle, join hands, and gently sway from right to left on the first pulse of each measure.

Translation

Oh, mama,
Oh, mama,
You left me alone
With my suffering.

TRAVELING

but <u>Not</u> in a Circle

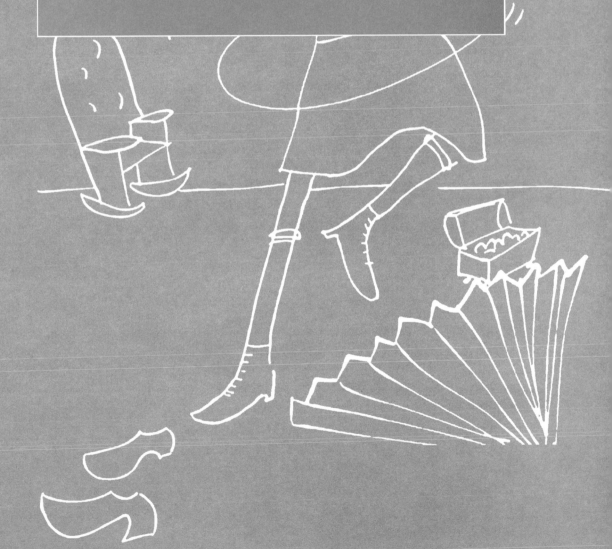

Allee Allee O

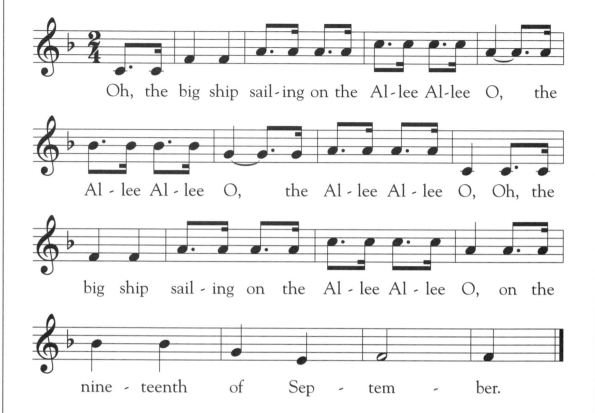

Oh, the big ship sail-ing on the Al-lee Al-lee O, the Al-lee Al-lee O, the Al-lee Al-lee O, Oh, the big ship sail-ing on the Al-lee Al-lee O, on the nine-teenth of Sep-tem-ber.

Motions

The children hold hands and form a line. The child at one end anchors the line by holding onto a wall or pole. The child at the other end leads the line (walking on the beat) under the arch formed by the anchor and the wall. After the entire line passes under the arch, the anchor (still holding onto the wall) turns 180 degrees and ends with his or her arms crossed in front. The leader then takes the line under the arch formed by the anchor and the person next to the anchor. When the entire line has passed under this arch, the person next to the anchor turns 180 degrees and ends with his or her arms crossed. The game continues as the line shrinks and the arch moves further away from the anchor with each repetition until the entire line is standing with arms crossed in front. The line then begins to unwind with the leader backing up through the last arch formed. Continue until the entire line has unwound.

All 'Round the Brickyard

All 'round the brick - yard,

Re - mem - ber me. I'm gon - na

step it, step it, step it and a -

re - mem - ber me.

Motions

The children take turns leading the group
around the room. The leader demonstrates
a motion and all those who follow copy
that motion as they travel.

Go 'Round the Mountain

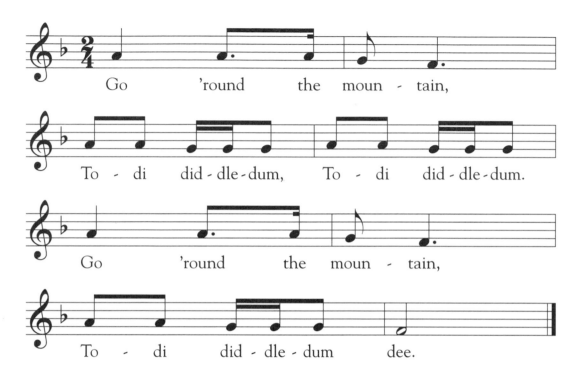

Go 'round the moun - tain,

To - di did - dle - dum, To - di did - dle - dum.

Go 'round the moun - tain,

To - di did - dle - dum dee.

During verse one, walk randomly around the room.

Verse 2

Show me your finger...

During verse two, stop near someone and shake your finger at that partner.

Verse 3

Select your partner...

During verse three, partners walk around holding hands. At the end of verse three, partners separate. Repeat the song from the beginning, searching for a new partner.

Hi-Di-Ho

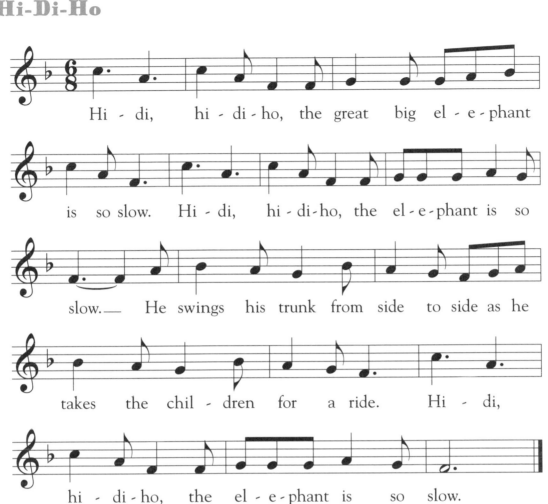

Hi - di, hi - di - ho, the great big el - e - phant

is so slow. Hi - di, hi - di - ho, the el - e - phant is so

slow.— He swings his trunk from side to side as he

takes the chil - dren for a ride. Hi - di,

hi - di - ho, the el - e - phant is so slow.

Motions

*The children walk around on the beat with
one arm hanging down (like an elephant's
trunk) and swinging back and forth with
the beat.*

How Do You Do-ti   *Australian*

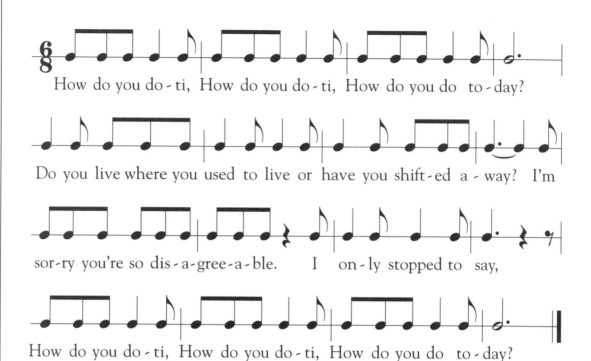

How do you do-ti, How do you do-ti, How do you do to-day?

Do you live where you used to live or have you shift-ed a-way? I'm

sor-ry you're so dis-a-gree-a-ble.   I   on-ly stopped to   say,

How do you do-ti, How do you do-ti, How do you do to-day?

Motions

Phrase 1: The group stands in a circle with arms crossed, holding the hand of the person on each side. Shake hands following the beat of the rhyme.

Phrase 2: Everyone switches, crossing arms with the other arm on top. Continue to shake hands following the beat of the rhyme.

Phrase 3: Everyone crosses arms as at the beginning. Continue to shake hands following the beat of the rhyme.

Phrase 4: Everyone walks randomly around the room. At the end of the phrase, reassemble in a circle with arms crossed ready to begin again.

As learned from Sanna Longden

I Love the Mountains

I love the moun-tains,   I love the roll-ing hills,

I love the foun-tains,   I love the daf-fo-dils,

I love the fi-re-side,   when— the lights are low.

Boom-di-a-da, boom-di-a-da, Boom-di-a-da, boom-di-a-da,

Boom-di-a-da, boom-di-a-da, Boom-di-a-da, boom-di-a-da,

Boom-di-boom, boom.

Motions

The children march with the beat while singing the song. The leader should lead the group around in a twisting and turning line, as in Follow the Leader.

May be sung as a four-part round.

Paige's Train

Pai - ge's   train   runs   so   fast,

Can't   see   noth - in'   but   the   win - dow   glass.

Verse 2

Paige's mule goes so slow,
There'll always be another row
    to hoe.

*Individuals take turns leading the group
around in a single line while performing
some motion. The group copies the leader's
motions and tempo.*

Snail, Snail

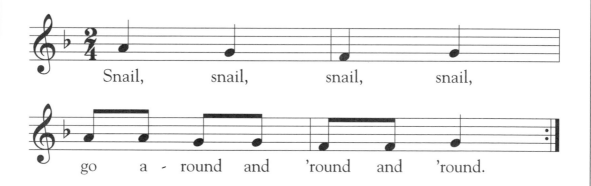

Snail,   snail,   snail,   snail,

go   a - round   and   'round   and   'round.

Motions

*Children hold hands in a circle. One
person (the leader) takes the line on an
inward spiral. After the line is well wound,
the leader takes everyone on an outward
spiral traveling between the rows of
children still on the inward spiral. The circle will end facing out. The line performs
another inward and outward spiral to bring
the children back to facing into the circle.*

Rig-a-Jig Jig

As I was walk-ing down the street, down the street,

down the street, A pret-ty friend I chanced to meet, Heigh-

ho, heigh-ho, heigh-ho. Rig-a-jig, jig and a-way we go,

way we go, way we go. Rig-a-jig, jig and a-

way we go, heigh-ho, heigh-ho, heigh-ho.

Motions

During the first half of the song, children randomly walk around the room stepping with the beat. During the second half of the song, children grab the hands of someone near and swing their partner's arms back and forth with the beat. As the song repeats, everyone leaves their partners. During the second half of the song, the children find new partners.

The Thread Follows the Needle

The thread fol - lows the nee - dle. The

thread fol - lows the nee - dle.

In and out the nee - dle goes, as

Moth - er mends the chil - dren's clothes.

Motions

The children hold hands and form a line. The child at one end anchors the line by holding onto a wall or pole. The child at the other end leads the line (walking on the beat) under the arch formed by the anchor and the wall. After the entire line passes under the arch, the anchor (still holding onto the wall) turns 180 degrees and ends with his or her arms crossed in front. The leader then takes the line under the arch formed by the anchor and the person next to the anchor. When the entire line has passed under this arch, the person next to the anchor turns 180 degrees and ends with his or her arms crossed. The game continues as the line shrinks and the arch moves further away from the anchor with each repetition until the entire line is standing with arms crossed in front. The line then begins to unwind with the leader backing up through the last arch formed. Continue until the entire line has unwound.

Turn, Cinnamon, Turn

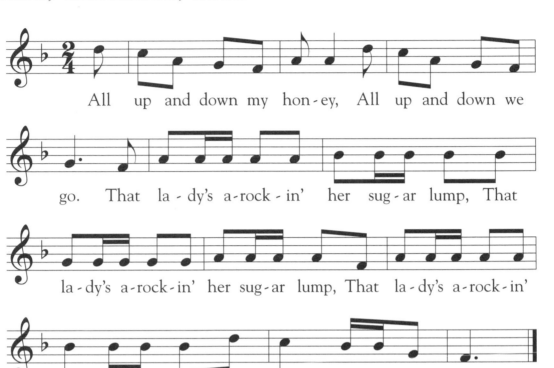

All up and down my hon-ey, All up and down we go. That la-dy's a-rock-in' her sug-ar lump, That la-dy's a-rock-in' her sug-ar lump, That la-dy's a-rock-in' her sug-ar lump, Oh, turn, cin-na-mon, turn.

Motions

The children sit randomly around on the floor. The leader (or teacher) begins singing and walking around the room. In the fourth measure, the leader picks another person, who then stands up. The pair holds both hands and swings them back and forth. They let go and turn around one time at, "Oh, turn, cinnamon, turn." Then, they both walk around and choose someone else with whom to swing arms. Continue until everyone is standing and then continue with each person picking a new partner on each repetition.

Wind Up the Apple Tree

Wind up the ap - ple tree,

Hold on tight,

Wind it all day and

Wind it all night.

Verse 2

Unwind the apple tree, hold on tight.
Unwind all day and unwind all night.

*Everyone forms a line and holds hands.
The leader takes the group on an inward
spiral until the line is tightly wound. Sing
the first verse as many times as is
necessary to accomplish this. During the
second verse, the leader takes the group in
the opposite direction, between the lines in
an outward spiral.*

Left! Left!

Left! Left!
I left my wife and forty-eight children,
Alone in the kitchen,
In starving condition
With nothing but gingerbread…
  (*Repeat from beginning*)

Someone leads the line of children in a twisting pathway. Begin marching on left foot. Continue, repeating poem without missing a beat.

Left, Left

Left, left,
I left my wife in New Orleans
With forty-five cents and a can of
  beans.
And I thought it was right, right,
Right for the country, whoopty doo!
(skipping step)

Begin marching on left foot. At "whoopty doo," all should do a quick right-left-right to shift back to the left foot in time for the next beat.

Off to Timbuktu

We are off to Timbuktu,
Would you like to go there too?
All the way and back again,
You must follow our leader then.
You must follow our leader,
You must follow our leader,
All the way and back again,
You must follow our leader.

Children take turns leading the group around the room. The leader initiates a motion and everyone else copies that motion as they travel around the room.

Polly Perkin

Polly Perkin,
Hold on to my jerkin,
Hold on to my gown.
That's the way we march to town.

Children take turns leading the group around the room. The leader initiates a motion and everyone else copies that motion as they travel around the room.

UnSquare Dancing

The teacher calls out the following directions while fiddle music or classical music is playing. Students walk around the room randomly and execute the moves as they are called.

Solo walk around the room.
Find a partner and swing 'em by the arm.
Swing that same partner with the other arm.

Solo walk around the room.
Find a new partner and promenade around.
Do-si-do that partner.

Solo walk around the room.
Find a partner for a right-hand 'round.
Take your partner and find another couple and circle to the right.

Solo walk around the room.
Find a partner for a left-hand 'round.
Take your partner and find another couple and circle to the left.

Solo walk around the room.
Find a new partner for a two-hand swing.
Take your partner and find another couple for a right-hand star.

Solo walk around the room.
Find a partner to promenade around.
Take your partner and find another couple and circle to the left.
Circle now the other way.
All step into the center and out again;
Into the center and out again.

Solo walk around the room.
Swing a partner by the arm.
Say goodbye and swing another.
Take your partner and find another couple.
All step into the center and stomp your foot, come on out and do it again.

Solo walk around the room.
Find a partner and do-si-do.
Take your partner and find another couple for a left-hand star.
Face your partner for the grand right and left.
Swing your partner when you meet 'em again.

Solo walk around the room.

TRAVELING
CIRCLE GAMES

All Around the Kitchen

Call: Response:

All a - round the kitch-en, Cock-a-doo-dle, doo-dle, doo.

All a - round the kitch-en, Cock-a - doo-dle, doo-dle, doo.

Now   stop right still, Cock-a - doo-dle, doo-dle, doo.

Put your hand on your hip, Cock-a - doo-dle, doo-dle, doo.

Let your right foot slip, Cock-a - doo-dle, doo-dle, doo.

Then   do it like this, Cock-a - doo-dle, doo-dle, doo.

All a - round the kitch-en, Cock-a-doo-dle, doo-dle, doo.

All a - round the kitch-en, Cock-a-doo-dle, doo-dle, doo.

All stand in a circle with one child in the middle.

Motions

All around the kitchen
Children walk in a circle.

Now stop right still
The circle stops.

Put your hand on your hip
All place right hand on hip.

Let your right foot slip
All circle to the right walking step-close, step-close.

Then do it like this
Child in the center demonstrates a repeated motion.

All around the kitchen
All perform the motion while moving to the right.

As the song repeats children walk in a circle and a new child is chosen to be in the center.

Coffee Grows on White Oak Trees

Cof - fee grows on white oak trees, the riv - er

flows with hon - ey - o, Go choose some - one to roam with

you, as sweet as m'las - ses can - dy - o.

(Two) in the mid - dle and you can't dance, Jo - sie,

(Two) in the mid - dle and you can't dance, Jo - sie,

(Two) in the mid - dle and you can't dance, Jo - sie,

Hel - lo Su - san Brown - i - o.

Motions

During the first half of the song, children walk around in a circle. One child walks around in the opposite direction. During the last half of the song, the one in the middle selects someone to join him or her. The two in the middle swing around by their right arms and then their left arms. The dance is repeated with two children walking around the inside of the circle. During the second half, the two in the center each choose a partner and swing that partner. Continue the dance, doubling the number of children in the center until there are "all in the middle."

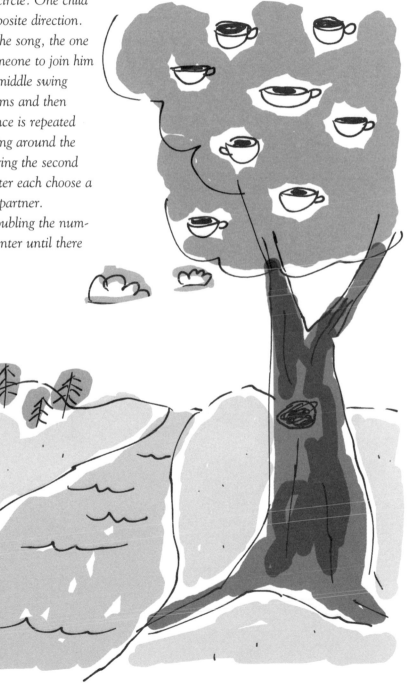

Green Gravel

Green grav - el, green grav - el, the grass is so green, The

fair - est young maid - en that ev - er was seen.

Verse 2

Miss (_____), Miss (_____),
Your true love is dead.
He sent you a letter
To turn back your head.

*During the first verse, all children walk in
a line, holding hands and stepping on the
beat. During the second verse, as each
child's name is sung (Miss _____ or
Mister _____), that person lets go of
his or her hands, turns 180 degrees, and
rejoins hands.*

Ida Red

I - da Red, I - da Red, I'm in love with I - da Red,

I - da Blue, I - da Blue, I'm in love with I - da Blue.

I - da Brown, I - da Brown, Hitched the horse and went to town.

I - da Black, I - da Black, Hitched him up and sent him back.

Motions

During the first half of the song, children walk around in a circle while one child walks in the opposite direction. During the last half of the song, the circle stands still and taps the beat on their legs while the child in the center selects another child and the two of them hold both hands and swing each other around. At the end of the song, the first child joins the circle and the song repeats with the new child walking in the opposite direction.

Jolly Is the Miller

Jol - ly is the mill - er that lives by the mill; — The
wheel turns a - round of its own free will. — With
one hand in the hop - per and the oth - er in the sack, — The
wheel turns a - round but the gents go back.

Motions

Children walk around in a circle in pairs,
holding hands. One child walks around the
inside of the circle in the opposite direction.
During the last phrase, the inside circle
moves forward to the next partner while the
outside circle waits for their new partner.
During this exchange, the one in the middle
"steals" someone's partner. The person left
without a partner is the next person to walk
around the inside of the circle.

O How Lovely Is the Evening

O how love-ly is the eve-ning, Is the eve-ning;

When the bells are sweet-ly ring-ing, sweet-ly ring-ing.

Ding Dong, Ding Dong, Ding Dong.

May be sung as a round.

Optional Dance

The class forms one large circle.

Phrase 1: Walk on the dotted quarter note to the left.

Phrase 2: Walk on the dotted quarter note to the right.

Phrase 3: Swing arms; out, in, out, in, out, in.

Dance as a Round

Form three concentric circles. Sing and dance as a round. Perform the entire song two times. After the final time, each group repeats the last phrase until everyone has finished. On the last "dong," all children hum the last note as they slowly lift their arms in a large circle (forward, up and down). As they lower their arms, the humming fades out.

Little Speck O' Lady

Leader: I'm a lit-tle speck o' la-dy, Group: Shoo! Shoo!

from 'cross the coun-try, Shoo! Shoo!

With a sil-ver nee-dle, Shoo! Shoo!

and a gold-en thim-ble. Shoo! Shoo!

O Miss Sal-ly Mae, Shoo! Shoo!

Fly a-way to the cor-ner. Shoo! Shoo!

Miss Clar-et-ta fol-low, Shoo! Shoo!

Fly a-way to the cor-ner. Shoo! Shoo!

Motions

Everyone holds hands in a circle with one girl in the center (only girls go to the center of the circle). The circle walks in one direction while the girl in the center walks in the opposite direction. At "O Miss Sally Mae," the circle stops and taps the beat on their legs while the girl picks another girl to swing by the right arm. At the end of the song, the new girl stays in the center and the first one returns to the circle.

O Sister Phoebe

O sis - ter Phoe - be, how mer - ry were we, The
night we sat un - der the ju - ni - per tree, The
ju - ni - per tree, hi - o, hi - o. The
ju - ni - per tree, hi - o.

Motions

During the first verse children walk around in a circle with one child in the middle. One of the children walking in the circle wears a hat.

Verse 2

Put this hat on your head to keep warm,
And one or two kisses will do you no harm,
Will do you no harm, hi-o, hi-o,
Will do you no harm, hi-o.

The child with the hat goes to the child in the center of the circle and places the hat on his or her head, then rejoins the circle that is still walking around.

Verse 3

Go choose you a partner, go choose you a one,
Go choose you the fairest that ever you can,
Now rise up you sister (brother), and go and go,
Now choose you a sister (brother) and go.

The child in the center chooses another. Holding hands, those two walk around the inside of the circle in the opposite direction the circle is walking. At the end of the verse, the child with the hat joins the walking circle and leaves the chosen child in the center.

Riding Here to Get Married

Rid - ing here to get mar - ried, Get

mar - ried, get mar - ried.

Rid - ing here to get mar - ried,

Ran - som a - tam - son a - cin - na - mon tea.

Motions

The children walk around in a circle in pairs forming two circles. At the end of the song, the children in the inner circle stay still while the children in the outer circle move forward to the next partner. Repeat the song until all children are back to their original partners.

Sallie Go 'Round

Sal - lie go 'round the sun,

Sal - lie go 'round the moon,

Sal - lie go 'round the chim - ney pot,

Ev - 'ry af - ter - noon.

Motions

Children walk around in a circle in one direction while one child walks around the inside of the circle in the opposite direction. At the end of the song, the child in the middle taps another child on the shoulder, and that child follows the first child around in the opposite direction for a few beats. The original child crouches down in the center of the circle while the second child continues walking in the opposite direction of the circle. At the end of the song, the second child chooses another to follow in the opposite direction. The song is repeated until only one child is walking around; all the other children are crouched down in the center. At the end of the last repetition, all children jump up and shout "BOOM!"

Somebody Waiting

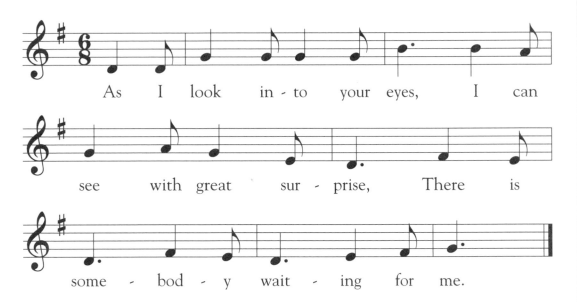

As I look in - to your eyes, I can see with great sur - prise, There is some - bod - y wait - ing for me.

Motions

The children walk around in a circle while one child (or more) walks around the inside of the circle in the opposite direction.

Verse 2

There is somebody waiting, there is
  somebody waiting,
There is somebody waiting for me.

The circle stops walking, and all tap with the beat on their legs. The child in the center continues to walk around the circle.

Verse 3

Choose two, leave the others, choose
  two, leave the others,
Choose two, leave the others for me.

Children in the circle continue to tap with the beat on their legs. The child in the

center selects two other children next to each other and forms a small circle of three. That group of three walk around in a circle where they are.

Verse 4

Swing one, leave the other, swing one,
  leave the other,
Swing one, leave the other for me.

The original child selects one of the two previously chosen children and swings that child by the arm in a circle. The other child goes back to the original circle and continues tapping with the beat on his or her legs with the others. At the end of this verse, the original child returns to the circle and the newly selected child starts the game again.

Tideo

Pass one win-dow, Ti-de-o. Pass two win-dows, Ti-de-o.

Pass three win-dows, Ti-de-o. Jin-gle at the win-dow, Ti-de-o.

Ti-de-o, Ti-de-o, Jin-gle at the win-dow, Ti-de-o.

Ti-de-o, Ti-de-o, Jin-gle at the win-dow, Ti-de-o.

Motions

During the first two phrases, children walk around in a circle while one child walks around the inside of the circle in the opposite direction. During the last two phrases, the circle stops walking and taps the beat on their legs. The child in the center chooses another child. Holding both hands, they lean back and swing around. At the end of the song, the original child returns to the circle, and the new child begins the game again.

Tulilule

(Bounce) a-round, tu-li-lu-le, (Bounce) a-round, tu-li-lu-le,

(Bounce) a-round, tu-li-lu-le, Tu-li-lu my dar-ling.

Motions

*Individuals suggest other ways to move
around the circle.*

Walk All Around

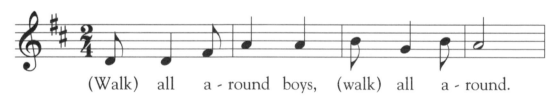

(Walk) all a-round boys, (walk) all a-round.

Eat so-da crack-ers, (walk) all a-round.

Motions

*The group walks around in a circle while
singing the song. Create other verses with
different motions to perform while traveling
around the circle.*

Dance and Sing Around the Ring *Shaker Tune*

Come dance and sing a - round the ring,

Live in love and un - ion,—

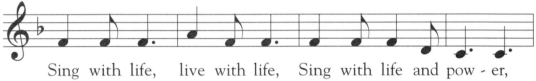

Dance and sing a - round the ring, Live in sweet com - mun - ion.

Sing with life, live with life, Sing with life and pow - er,

Sing with life, live with life, Sing with life and pow - er.

Motions

*The group holds hands and walks in a
circle while singing the song. One person
breaks the circle and leads everyone
spiraling in and then out. The energy,
volume, and tempo gradually increase.*

Walk Along John

Come on friends, and hush your talk - ing,

All join hands and let's go (walk - ing).

(Walk) a - long John with your pa - per col - lar on.

(Walk) a - long John with your pa - per col - lar on.

Motions

Individuals suggest other ways to move around the circle.

Tepok Amai-Amai (Ladybug) *Malaysian*

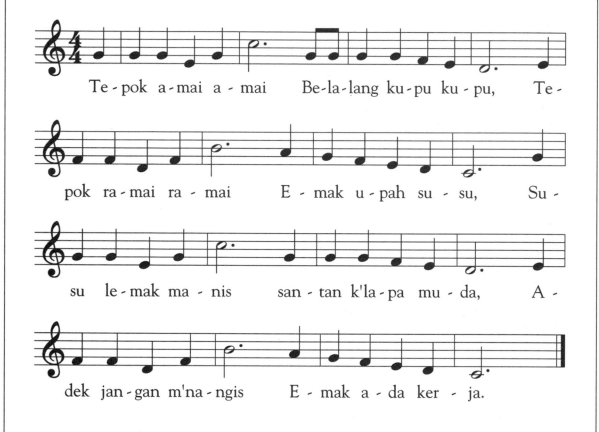

Te - pok a - mai a - mai   Be - la - lang ku - pu ku - pu,   Te -

pok ra - mai ra - mai   E - mak u - pah su - su,   Su -

su le - mak ma - nis   san - tan k'la - pa mu - da,   A -

dek jan - gan m'na - ngis   E - mak a - da ker - ja.

Motions

The group forms a circle. During the song, the children clap and step to the pulse, moving to the right. As Malaysian teachers do, cue the children (visually or with a tap on a drum) to clap twice as fast or twice as slow while singing the same speed.

Translation

Clap, little ladybugs, grasshoppers, and colorful butterflies.
Clap, everyone.
Mother will give you coconut milk, rich and sweet,
The sweetest coconut milk from the young fruits.
Little brother, don't cry.
Mother has work to do.

SIMPLE
DANCES

Four in a Boat

Four in a boat and the tide rose high,

Four in a boat and the tide rose high,

Four in a boat and the tide rose high,

Wait-ing for a pret-ty one to come by and by.

Motions

Children walk around in a circle in pairs with one child walking around in the opposite direction. (This game must be played with an odd number of children.) At the end of the song, the children in the outer ring stay still, and those in the inner ring move forward to a new partner. The child in the center takes this opportunity to "steal" someone's partner. The one left without a partner goes to the center and the game is repeated.

Great Big House

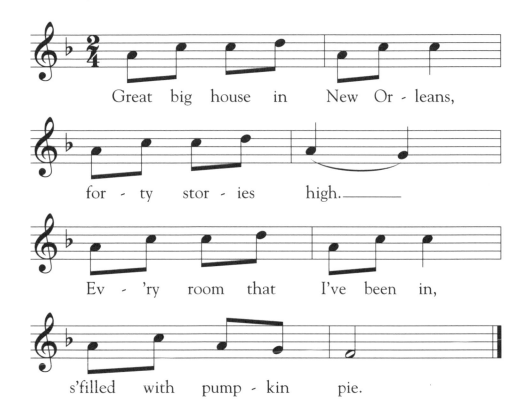

Great big house in New Or - leans,

for - ty stor - ies high.

Ev - 'ry room that I've been in,

s'filled with pump - kin pie.

Children stand in a circle; count off A or B.
All walk around in a circle.

Verse 2

Went down to the old mill stream,
   Every other child (A's) takes four steps into
   the circle and holds hands.
To fetch a pail of water.
   The other children (B's) take four steps into
   the circle and hold hands.
Put one arm around my wife,
   The A's lift their arms over, around and down
   behind the B's.

The other 'round my daughter.
   The B's lift their arms over, around and
   down behind the A's

Verse 3

Fare thee well my darling girl,
Fare thee well my daughter,
Fare thee well my darling girl,
With gold slippers on her.
   All walk around the circle with arms
   interwoven.

Pop Goes the Weasel

All a-round the cob-bler's bench, the mon-key chased the wea-sel.

The mon-key thought 'twas all— in fun. Pop, goes the wea-sel.

A pen-ny for a spool of thread, a pen-ny for a nee-dle.

That's the way the mon-ey goes. Pop, goes the wea-sel.

Motions

Phrases 1 & 2: Children walk around the circle in sets of three.

Phrase 3: Children continue walking while the outside children in each set of three join hands in front of the middle child.

Phrase 4: The children who are holding hands lift them to form an arch. The middle child passes under and moves to the next arch.

Continue the game until the children return to their original sets of three.

Seven Jumps   *Denmark*

Motions

Children make quick steps around in a circle for the first two phrases. During the first three notes of the third phrase children stomp three times, during the first three notes of the fourth phrase children clap three times. With the first fermata, children get down on one knee. With the second fermata, children bring the other knee down. Repeat from the beginning.

With each repeat of the dance, add one more fermata with the following motions:

3. Add one elbow.
4. Add the other elbow.
5. Add one hand flat on the floor.
6. Add the other hand flat on the floor.
7. Lay flat on the floor (or place head on the floor).

Three Jolly Fishermen

There were three jol - ly fish - er - men and they put out to

sea.— There were three jol - ly fish - er - men and

they put out to sea.— They threw their nets in -

to the sea and drew them out by one, two, three. To

see what they had got, had got, To see what they had got.—

Motions

During the first two phrases children walk around in a circle while three children are in the middle walking in the opposite direction. During the last two phrases the circle stops and the three go their own ways, select a child from the circle and swing him or her around by one arm. At the end of the song the original three join the outer circle, and the new children go to the center to begin the game again.

Weevily Wheat

Don't want your weev'-ly wheat, Don't want your bar-ley,

Take some flour for half an hour and bake a cake for Char-lie.

Five times five is twen-ty five, five times six is thir-ty,

five times sev'n is thir-ty five, five times eight is for-ty.

Motions

Groups of four students should make a circle. They should count off 1, 2, 3, 4 in order (going clockwise).

Phrase 1: Children walk around in one direction.

Phrase 2: Children turn and walk in the other direction.

Phrase 3: Child 1 puts his/her right hand out, palm down. Child 2 does the same, placing his or her right hand on top of the right hand of Child 1. Child 3 and then

Child 4 do the same, respectively. Child 1 adds his or her left hand to the pile, and Child 2, 3, and 4 do the same in order. This is done with the beat.

Phrase 4: The child whose hand is at the bottom pulls out his or her hand and puts it on top, and so on. This is done with the beat.

Index

Aiken Drum	34		Farmer, The	22
Al Citron	74		Fiddlers Playing	25
Ali Baba	64		Four in a Boat	132
All 'Round the Brickyard	99		Frog in the Meadow	29
All Around the Kitchen	112			
All Fools Day	84		Go 'Round the Mountain	100
All the Birds	84		Great Big House	133
Allee Allee O	98		Green Gravel	116
Ambos a Dos	10			
A Quackadilioso	80		Haul Away Joe	17
Aserrín	35		Head and Shoulders, Baby	51
			Hearts	85
Baroque and Blue	90		Here Comes Missis Macaroni	60
Betty Botter	84		Hey, Betty Martin	12
Bling, Blang	36		Hickory, Dickory, Dock	26
Blow the Wind	91		Hi-Di-Ho	101
Bryan O'Lin	90		How Do You Do-ti	102
Buzz	64			
			I Can Hammer	37
Checkerberry	79		I Dropped My Dolly	87
Cinderella	84		I Give You a Cat	75
Circle 'Round the Zero	56		I Love the Mountains	103
Cobbler, Cobbler	30		I Pass the Shoe	76
Cockles and Mussels	92		Ida Red	117
Coffee Grows on White Oak Trees	114			
Cup, Stick & Stone Passing	73		Jerry Hall	85
			Jigama, Jigama	64
Dame Get Up	11		Johnny Had One Friend	38
Dance and Sing Around the Ring	128		Johnny Works with One Hammer	39
Did You Ever See a Lassie?	14		Jolly Is the Miller	118
Do, Do, Pity My Case	15			
Doctor Fell	84		King William	87
Doctor Knickerbocker I	58		Kite, A	85
Doctor Knickerbocker II	59		Kye Kye, Kule	40
Down in the Valley	16			
Down on the Banks			Left! Left!	109
of the Hanky Panky	79		Left, Left	109
Draw Me a Bucket of Water	57		Listen, Listen	29
Ducky Duddles	85		Little Guinea Pig	85
			Little Johnny Brown	61
Engine, Engine	26		Little Speck O' Lady	120

Man of Words, A	86	Somebody Waiting	125
Minister's Cat, The	65	St. Dunstan	86
Minka	88	St. Paul's Steeple	86
Money Spent	86	Stick, Stick	72
Monkey Stomps His Feet, The	23		
Moses Supposes	90	Take It	79
Mother Goonie Bird	41	Tepok Amai-Amai (Ladybug)	130
My Aunt Came Back	42	Terence McDiddler	90
My Mother Sent Me Unto You	18	There's a Cobbler	31
My Name Is Joe	51	This Is a Pencil	73
My Ship Sailed from China	43	Thread Follows the Needle, The	106
		Three Bears, The	47
Neighbor, Neighbor	65	Three Jolly Fishermen	136
Nievie, Nievie	66	Tideo	126
		Tortillitas	49
O How Lovely Is the Evening	119	Tulilule	127
O Sister Phoebe	122	Turn, Cinnamon, Turn	107
Obwisana	77	'Twas on a Monday Morning	50
Off to Timbuktu	109	Tweedle, Tweedle	67
Oh, Dear	93		
Old Aunt Kate	89	Una Vieja	86
Old Mother Goose	90	UnSquare Dancing	110
Old Obidiah	62		
One Finger, One Thumb	44	Walk All Around	127
		Walk Along John	129
Paige's Train	104	Wash the Dishes	52
Parrot, A	86	Washer Woman	95
Peter Pumpkin Eater	86	Way Down Yonder	68
Pizza, Pizza	63	We're Gonna Go on a Bear Hunt	52
Polly Perkin	109	Wee Melody Man	70
Pop Goes the Weasel	134	Weevily Wheat	137
Puncinella	19	Well, A	90
		When I Was a Shoemaker	27
Riding Here to Get Married	123	Where, Oh, Where	78
Riding in a Buggy	45	Who Stole the Cookie	
Rig-a-Jig Jig	105	from the Cookie Jar?	49
Rock Candy	20	Who's the Leader?	66
		William He Had Seven Sons	28
Sallie Go 'Round	124	Wind Up the Apple Tree	108
San Serení	46	Wise Old Owl	86
Santa Maloney	21	Wishy Washy	71
Schumann Lullaby Op. 124, No. 6	94	Wonder Ball, The	73
Seven Jumps	135		
Shoe Our Pony	86	Yo, Mamana, Yo (Oh, Mama, Oh)	96
Sing at the Table	90		
Snail, Snail	104	Zodio	53